MW00653455

It seemed like a good idea at the time!

To my dad,
Nicholas Horodowich

Who taught me,

"You can always take it off,
but you can never put it on."

Practicing Good Judgment

Adventurer's Guide to Making Critical Decisions

By

Wayne Nicholas Horodowich

The University of Sea kayaking, LLC assumes no responsibility for accidents, incidents or injuries sustained by readers who use the information in this book.

First Printing: 2019

ISBN 978-0-9833299-4-7 (sc)
ISBN 978-1-6847038-2-1 (e)

University of Sea Kayaking, LLC
PO Box 12249
Mill Creek, WA 98082

www.useakayak.org
study@useakayak.org

You can order on-line from the USK Store via www.useakayak.org

Ordering Information:
Special discounts are available on quantity purchases by corporations, associations, educators, and others. For details, contact the publisher at the above listed address.

U.S. trade bookstores and wholesalers: Please contact University of Sea Kayaking, LLC via email study@useakayak.org

Printed in the United States of America

Cover Photo (Tetons) and all others by M & W Photography
Native Folk Drawings by Derek Charles Hutchinson
Illustrations and stamps by Wayne Horodowich

Rev.date: 08/12/2019

CONTENTS

Foreword vii

Preface ....,.. x

Acknowledgements xii

Introduction xiv

1- Judgment 1

2 – Decision-Making Lens 4

3 – Decision-Making Process (Reactive) 39

4 – Decision-Making Process (Proactive) 63

5 - Course of Action Scenarios 75

6 - Scenario Reviews 83

7 - Risk Assessment 123

8 - What to Know Before You Go 129

9 - Leaders - Participants - Groups 143

10 - Parting Thoughts 160

Appendices

    1. Packing Lists 163

    2. Minimizing Strong Emotions 169

    3. Decision I Wish I Could Change 172

Index 174

About the Author 179

When you come to the fork in the road,

take it!

-Yogi Berra

FOREWORD

The seed that blossomed into my love of the outdoors was planted by my Dad. Through him, I learned how to camp, fish, hunt and merely enjoy the natural world around me. Most importantly I learned to respect the outdoors, I learned how to enjoy it safely and I learned how being mentally prepared is even more important than having proper equipment and knowing how to use it.

That love and understanding of the outdoors continued to grow and my lessons expanded with my environments: through many primitive campouts while in the Boy Scouts, and then later as I earned a degree in Forestry. It rose to higher levels still when I moved to Alaska, settling on Kodiak Island, in the mid 80s.

I developed a small kayak touring business in Kodiak and began learning more about maritime safety and the survival skills required throughout the North Pacific coastal environment. Taught by US Coast Guard survival training personnel, and gleaned from fellow members of our Search and Rescue team who were part of the US Navy SEAL training unit based in Kodiak, I took every opportunity to learn about being outdoor self-reliant and safety and survival conscious in this demanding maritime environment.

I became a member of the Trade Association of Sea Kayaking, and for many years attended their West Coast Sea Kayak Symposium - at first as a sea kayaker/kayak tour operator, and then as a presenter on topics such as: self-reliance and kayak safety. It's also where I met Wayne Horodowich. Within minutes of our introduction, we formed a friendship bond that has lasted over 30 years and we still see eye-to-eye, figuratively *and* literally.

Wayne and I are both a lofty 6' 7", so it was always easy for us to quickly spot each other upon arrival at the event each year. Being rather tall for sea kayaking, we both had similar requirements for our gear of choice. We'd often compare notes and scout out boats and gear that would fit us. Mostly we were both there because we loved kayaking.

All of my life experiences and associations formed a solid foundation of knowledge and resources for when I began to dabble in freelance writing. My strong suit was kayaking and the skills one needs to be a responsible and accomplished paddler. From the start, Wayne has been my "go to" guy to make sure I was on the right track, or to reassure me that my information and suggestions were well grounded. I soon developed a solid basis upon which my "outdoor" writing would be founded: focus on "why" a particular technique or process is important, not merely "how it's done", but why should it be done this way. My intent was to inspire my readers to start thinking about what they were doing as it related to the goal or purpose of a particular process and not merely mimicking some routine they picked up from ambiguous media.

When Wayne asked me to review his manuscript, I happily said yes because I was already quite familiar and impressed with the great work he had done on his award-winning "In-Depth" Instructional Video Series for sea kayakers, as well as the numerous articles he has written for both his and other websites, and magazines.

As a working freelancer I am frequently engaged in penning outdoor skill and safety articles for several columns I write, along with a few websites to which I contribute. I was immediately intrigued by his proposed title, *Practicing Good Judgment*. Having been a professional guide, instructor, and author of a self-reliance/survival book, I understand the importance and complexities of trying to make quality, responsible decisions in the outdoors.

While reviewing Wayne's manuscript I was continually impressed by the way in which he explained the decision-making process. Because I write about this very subject, it inspired me to review my own judgment processes and reflect upon how and why I make the decisions I do.

Working through the many realistic scenarios Wayne included in the book gave me a chance to practice using his decision-making process. Doing so gave me an opportunity to reaffirm the criteria I use (or need to consider) when having to make tough calls.

Other components of judgment addressed in this book include: the concepts of adventure; risk and being safe; considerations for leaders; participants and group decision-making; and perhaps most important - what you need to know before you go out on your next adventure.

Reading **Practicing Good Judgment** will motivate you to re-examine your own decision-making process, and hopefully lead you towards making the best decisions possible in the future. It's a learning tool for those who are taking on the responsibility of leading others in a variety of outdoor adventure pursuits. Furthermore, even if you are not big on adventuring, it is still an invaluable reference for anyone seeking to become a more competent and responsible participant. No matter how you might be venturing forth, you will still find this book useful because you are making decisions everyday - and that process is the same regardless of your surroundings.

- Tom Watson, March 2019
(www.TomOutdoors.com)

PREFACE

Wouldn't if be great if you had a ready-to-use solution for every situation that comes your way, so it could be said you showed good judgment? Unfortunately, it is not possible because there are too many unknown circumstances that need to be considered in order to do so. Not that we haven't tried. In reality, there are numerous standard responses we have in our daily routines and ones we have been taught for emergencies. Take CPR as an example. The training focuses on calling for help and then the few steps to follow until that more qualified assistance arrives. Your job is to try and keep oxygen flowing to the victim's brain through mouth-to-mouth resuscitation and external chest compressions. Other than the safety of your immediate surroundings, nothing else needs to be considered. This is a set response to a very specific situation.

Those of us who love outdoor adventures do so in an ever-changing environment, making it impossible to have a ready-to-go, in-the-box response for all the possible situations that could arise during our outing. That means we have to make critical decisions on the spot. Here is just one example. What would you do in this situation? Really try to see yourself in this canyon and answer as truthfully as possible.

You are a leader of a youth group with five 6th graders in your charge and the six of you are hiking in the upper remote canyons of Zion Canyon National Park. The sun is still out even though the afternoon forecast is for thunderstorms in the area. You and the kids are in a narrow canyon when you hear faint sounds of thunder off in the distance but you still have sun above you.

Fifteen minutes later you start to hear a roaring sound that seems to be getting louder. You realize a flash flood is coming at you and your group. You know you cannot out run the flood so you look for higher ground. You usher the youngsters into a side crevice that seems to be going uphill. You climb as high as you can until you reach a 12- foot high wall. You can see that the crevice keeps going up beyond the wall at a gradual angle. Knowing you are tall enough you know you can boost the kids up over the ledge since they cannot do it on their own. The water is rising up to your location and the children are scared. The last one in line slips back and is washed downstream. What is your course of action? Do you jump in after the one child and leave the four or stay with the four and accept the loss of the one?

Before you continue reading make a definitive decision. Now that you have made your decision would that decision change if the one child who fell in happens to be your son or daughter? Do you jump in due to parental instincts? Do you let your child go and take care of the remaining 4 children? Again try to be as honest as possible when you answer.

This is a horrific - yet possible scenario. Regardless of what you do, you are going to be judged harshly by your spouse, family and by the families of the youngsters in your charge, if you live through the ordeal. You will also be judged by anyone who hears about this incident on the 6 o'clock news, which will be seen across North America and possibly in world news.

There is a lot to consider when we make decisions, especially difficult or life threatening ones. After reading this book I want you to come back to this scenario to see if you would answer it differently. This scenario, and many others will be reviewed later in the book.

ACKNOWLEDGEMENTS

Since the information I am sharing in this book and all of my actions in my life are based upon my collective experiences, I want to share appreciation to all of you who have contributed to who I am today. Needless to say there are too many of you to mention, even if I could remember you all. Of course there have been many standouts, some of whom I am including below.

I want to thank the following for their direct and indirect contributions to this book: my three adventure buddies (Lee Carter (who taught me right and wrong have nothing to do with the law), Paul Carty (who taught me the value of a red sweatshirt) and Dr. Tom Lionvale (who demonstrated what NOT to eat in the outdoors or anywhere else)), Don Snider (for his wisdom and guidance), Jon Spaventa (for his support and political acumen), my UCSB Adventure Program assistants who helped develop and grow the program (Maureen O'Hagan, Sonja Hodges-Martin (Big "S") and Rod Tucknott), the Adventure Program instructors-staff-leaders & participants (for all of the lessons we learned together), Outward Bound Schools (for introducing me to a new life and recognizing self-imposed limits), Dick Rice (for his thoughts on risk and adventure), MF (for demonstrating the value of patience), Derek C. Hutchinson (for his original native artwork and being a friend, devil's advocate & mentor), my sister Cathe T. (who, at age five, taught me, "when enough - is enough" by chasing me out of the apartment with a baseball bat) and to my parents Nick & Nadja Horodowich (for instilling sound values, teaching me to take responsibility for my mistakes, to never give up and it is okay to cry).

Brooklyneeze is my primary language. Therefore, I want to thank Becky Hardey for her keen eye in editing my manuscript. She is not only an avid reader; she is an accomplished adventurer in her own right.

Last and certainly not least, is a very special thank you to Tom Watson - a dear member of my tribe. His help in editing this book has been invaluable to me. As a professional adventure writer and guide, Tom's suggestions helped make this book stronger. Check out his website (TomOutdoors.com) to see some of his works.

INTRODUCTION

I know you have been making decisions your entire life and are probably doing just fine. I am guessing there were times when you were told you showed both good judgment and poor judgment. If it was good, you felt proud. If it wasn't, it probably hurt a little or a lot, depending on who was telling you.

Have you ever really thought about your own judgment? Regardless of your age, it is always worthwhile to do a self-examination of how and why you do things. I have written this book for exactly that purpose. The contents within will help you clarify your judgment and provide ways to improve your decision-making process, with the goal of being better than "just fine."

As an instructor/guide trainer I have had numerous discussions with my peers regarding student training. During those discussions I often heard other trainers say, you can teach skills but you cannot teach judgment. In my early days as a trainer I agreed with that statement. However it was during a 20-hour drive from Port Townsend, Washington, to Santa Barbara, California, when I began thinking about teaching judgment.

At that time I was the director of Adventure Programs at the University of California, Santa Barbara (UCSB). While in that position I developed a Leadership Training Course where I, along with the rest of my staff, trained college students to be outdoor guides and instructors. As I drove along, I was thinking of the students I had trained and I asked myself if I could indeed, trust their judgment. Not only was I training them, I was sending them out on trips leading others on outdoor adventures. Due to my standards, I would not send a leader out unless I believed I trusted their judgment.

The bulk of my staff training was skill based and involved taking them on the trips that they could eventually be leading. Part of the process was teaching by example.

Covering emergency contingencies was also included. When I chose the staff to lead trips, I picked the ones who impressed me most when I viewed them in action. I was using my judgment of their performance. As I thought about their judgment, I wondered if they had learned it through my course or had they brought it with them? If I did teach it to them, how was I doing it?

That question piqued my curiosity; it made me think about the skill training I was doing and the realization that I had no clear and proactive training for "judgment." My mind quickly moved onto the idea of teaching judgment. Can it be taught? Can it be learned? Since I believe the answer to both questions is yes, my next question was, "How can I formalize it in my training as a specific subject?" I knew I'd have a lot of research and thinking to do about the subject when I got home.

Let's face the truth. When it comes down to it, just because someone is trained in skills and/or judgment, it does not guarantee they will perform when the time comes. Even if they demonstrate their capabilities when being evaluated, all you can say is, on that particular day, they successfully demonstrated their ability to perform. In reality, that is all any certification can verify. It cannot predict future behavior. However, the chances are significantly greater that you will get the expected performance from individuals who are trained, in contrast to those who are not.

During the year following that long ride I began to develop a method for teaching judgment, which would add another dimension to our training program. Over the years, my experience in trying to teach judgment has evolved to sharing it at different symposia and professional outdoor events. This book is the culmination of all my experience in the arena of teaching judgment.

My five main goals in this book are:
- Identify what is meant by judgment;

- Take a close look at the many factors you use in your judgment;
- Describe the decision-making process;
- Provide you with exercises/scenarios to practice your decision-making process;
- Review mistakes made by others in order to help you from repeating them.

I am writing this book for my fellow adventurers, or as I lovingly refer to, "My tribe." We are the ones who like to recreate and challenge ourselves in and around Mother Nature. However, the concepts contained in this book are for **EVERYONE** because we all use our judgment every day. The major difference is, the outdoor environment often times has greater consequences when we show poor judgment.

No single book can tell you what to do in every situation because there are too many possibilities. What I can do is provide you with a solid foundation for you to use when you have to decide what to do. As I mentioned earlier, just because you may know what to do, doesn't mean you will do it when the time comes. All I can do is show you the process and how to use it. In my experience, those who have learned and utilized the concepts within this book have been able to make better decisions during their adventures.

*"Most people mean well,
some just don't know what 'well' means."*

-Leonard Watson

CHAPTER 1

JUDGMENT

In the introduction I mentioned my initial thoughts on judgment during my twenty-hour drive. When I got home I immediately started my quest regarding teaching this subject. To help me clarify my thought process I went to my Webster's dictionary. As with any dictionary definition there are several meanings depending upon the context in which the word is being used.

Definitions of Judgment:
1. A formal utterance of an authoritative opinion;
2. A formal **decision** given by a court;
3. A final judging of mankind by God;
4. The process of forming an **opinion** or evaluation by discerning and comparing;
5. A position stating something believed or asserted.

In the frame of reference in which I was thinking about judgment, the words *opinion* and *decision* jumped out at me. Your judgment is your <u>opinion</u>, the basis used, in your <u>decision</u> to take an action. It became suddenly clear, that teaching judgment needs to focus on the criteria or the reasoning one uses to make decisions and the decision-making process (**DMP**).

When thinking about the criteria we use, I tried to find a better way to label it other than judgment, because of the other definitions there are for the word. As an example, when the judge rendered their ruling, based upon their judgment, it was a final judgment, which I thought showed poor judgment.

It can get confusing sometimes and my goal is to clarify the process. Instead of using "judgment," I decided to use "decision-making lens," which will be explained in greater detail in the next chapter.

Good & Poor Judgment

When I thought more about our concerns as trainers, I realized we were using the wrong words when lamenting that judgment can't be taught. Any time one of our students made a decision and acted on it, they were using judgment, so we were really questioning what kind of judgment our trainees use. Once **they** made their decision, using their personal criteria, we would use *our* own factors to assess *their* action deciding if it was a "good" or "poor" one. Therefore, what we were really saying was, "You cannot teach **good** judgment."

During my "teaching judgment" lecture I use the following scenario to illustrate the ambiguity of good & poor judgment:

I've taken Ben and Mary in the outdoors for a training session. The conditions become life threatening and I have to make a choice of saving either Ben or Mary because I cannot save both. If I save Mary most likely her family will say I showed good judgment. Ben's family will likely say I showed poor judgment. Who is right?

From yet another perspective, my outdoor professional peers will likely say I showed poor judgment by getting into that situation in the first place. Again, who is right?

Since "good" and "poor" are a matter of opinion and can be a no-win battle, I chose to put my energies towards developing a teachable process. I firmly believe the last thing any outdoor professional or practitioner should be thinking about is caring more about the opinions of others over the well-being of those in their charge. I prefer my trip leaders to act decisively, based on a well-thought-out process using sound reasoning.

Whether you are an outdoor professional, a day hiker, a scout leader, a backpacker, a paddler or any other adventurer, you should understand the **DMP** and the factors in your **Lens** upon which you're making your decisions. Since this process is used everyday for every decision you

2

make - regardless of your environment - you should be well aware of it.

The Armchair Quarterback

Anyone who has observed a passionate football fan knows what I am talking about when I reference the "armchair quarterback." As they watch the game they are shouting at the quarterback's image on the screen, telling them what they should be doing. While I admire the passion, I have to laugh! How do you imagine that same fan would fare if he or she were actually down on the field, tired and beat up by the third quarter with a massive human wall of muscle bearing down on them with *"I am going to obliterate you"* in their eyes?

It's much easier to sit back and judge the actions of others when you are not in the actual situation you find yourself judging. There are oftentimes many unreported aspects well beyond what we read regarding outdoor incidents. Some decisions may have required a split-second decision. Any decisions you make while nestled in a cozy chair in the comfort of your home may be very different if you were struggling in a snowstorm and forced to make a life or death decision while being cold, hungry and fatigued.

I am making this point for two reasons: First, for the armchair quarterback, do not be too quick to judge from the comfort and security of your home and realize you will never have all the facts; and second, for the person taking the action, do not worry about the armchair quarterbacks of the world. Do what you think is best given the situation. In the end you have to live with the consequences of your actions, whether good or bad, regardless of what others are saying about you.

CHAPTER 2

DECISION-MAKING LENS

Every decision you make in your life is based upon some sort of reasoning. As I mentioned in the previous chapter, I am referring to that reasoning as your "Decision-Making Lens." Your lens is more than your reasoning; it is how you view and choose to respond to the world around you.

My Webster's dictionary defines a lens as something that facilitates and influences perception, comprehension or evaluation.

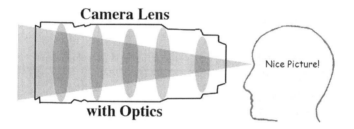

If you look at the design of a camera lens you will see why I am using it as an example, my metaphor, to explain how we view the world. A camera lens is comprised of different glass optics. Each individual glass optic has a different purpose but all of them together comprise the lens with the goal of providing you a specific image. A high percentage of the time an effective decision is based on multiple factors, not just one. It's those different factors, when combined, instead of optics, that become your decision-making lens.

When it comes to making decisions, your **"lens"** is at the heart of every step of the **D**ecision-**M**aking **P**rocess (DMP). Without some sort of rationale (your lens-factors) you could not make a decision. The richness and depth of your factors will determine the effectiveness of your decision.

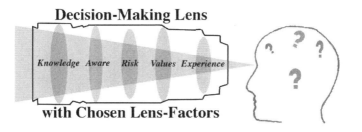

Decision-Making Lens

Knowledge Aware Risk Values Experience

with Chosen Lens-Factors

Your lens-factors comprise everything you've experienced in your life. It is ever changing, ever evolving, every minute, every second you are alive. What you know today will change as you learn. What you believe today can change for any number of reasons. Even though your factors are dynamic, when you do use them in your lens they are the total of your life's experience up to that very moment of use. In fact, as your lens-factors change, the decision you make today may be different if you had to make the same decision a week later. The key point is that your lens-factors are always evolving.

Lens-Factors

Each of us will have our own list of lens-factors that we can put into our decision-making lens. Below is a list of the significant factors in my arsenal. Your factors may be similar, but I believe everyone's list will have some differences. What is important is for you to know your list. Rather than just reading mine, I encourage you to create you own list, which will give you a better understanding of your DMP.

Factors I use in my decision-making lens (Not all, but the ones used most often):

- *Beliefs* – Information, details and things I hold true;
- *Values* - Ideals, traits and beliefs I hold in high regard and/or esteem;
- *Emotions* – How I feel (calm, scared, angry, grieving, etc);
- *Drive* - Energy and motivation used for action;
- *Ego* – How I view myself;
- *Reputation* – How others view me;

- **Desires** - Wants, hopes & dreams;
- **Others** - How it will affect others and the environment;
- **Expectations** - Assurances and anticipation;
- **Preferences** – What I like better or give priority;
- **Awareness** – Viewing self, others and the environment;
- **Experience** – What I have learned in life by doing;
- **Knowledge** – Sum total of my learning;
- **Skills** – Physical knowledge gained through training (versus intellectual knowledge);
- **Commitments** – Promises & obligations to others;
- **Regulations** – Laws, rules and policies;
- **Physical status** – External conditioning;
- **Physiological status** – Internal body functions (cold, hot, hungry, tired, strong, weak, dehydrated, etc);
- **Psychological status** – Behavioral and/or personal issues;
- **Risk assessment** – Perceiving, evaluating & matching to abilities;
- **Time** – Time and timing
- **Money** - Price and financial value
- **Future hindsight** – Looking ahead to look back;
- **Gut feeling** – Inner voice.

It is important to understand these factors and how they can affect your DMP. The more you know about your factors, the more confident you will be in your decisions. Let's review each lens-factor to get a more in-depth understanding of these factors and how they can affect your decisions. I've included specific examples (*in italics*) that I have witnessed and/or had to deal with that help illustrate my points.

    Beliefs - My Webster's Dictionary defines "belief "as a conviction of the truth of some statement or reality. You perceive your beliefs are true; otherwise they would NOT be beliefs. However, just because you think they are true does not make it fact. I am willing to wager that many times in your life you have had beliefs that were not true, but at the time you would swear they were indeed true. Once you found a new truth it may have changed your initial belief. Since your beliefs can change as you go through life, it means the decisions you make today may be different from those of tomorrow for the same event.

It is important to mention that your religious/spiritual beliefs can be very powerful in making decisions. I include this because attached to many of these beliefs are strong commitments and strict rules.

During my Outward Bound Mountaineering Course in Oregon's Three Sister Wilderness area we had an episode in my patrol where we had a strong disagreement as to our location. I believed one thing and others believed something else. Their belief meant losing 1,000 feet and then gaining that elevation back when taking their route. My belief meant a few hundred feet of gain from our location and less miles than their option to our final destination. We were each holding strongly to our beliefs. The only way to find out the truth was to choose one. Luckily I was able to convince the group to let me climb to the ridge and signal them if I was correct. It worked out that I was correct and we saved a lot of energy that day. Since all of us were new to reading contour maps (topo' maps), I could have been the one who was wrong. Opposing beliefs or any other opposing factors in your lens can cause difficulties in your process or in a group when decisions need to be made.

Values - These are the ideals, traits and beliefs you hold in high regard and/or esteem. Since most people try to live their lives according to their values, it is important you spend time identifying yours. Is one life more important than ten? What if that one was your child's and you had to choose between their life and ten strangers? I offer these two examples so you can start thinking about some of your values.

I once attended a lecture at an Association of Experiential Education (AEE) Conference on value clarification. The speaker opened the lecture by saying "a value is not a value until you live it." Later that night, as I sat in my hotel room reviewing my notes, I realized the implications of that opening remark. Instead of listing my perceived values, I made a list of how I lived my life because these are my lived values. I have to say I was not proud of some of the actions on my list. It was very clear there was a discrepancy between my stated and lived values.

It is easier to state your values when you don't have to live them. I challenge you to be honest with yourself and list your perceived and lived values. If they don't match, you have some reconciling to do. You can either change your stated values to how you live your life or change your life to try to live up to what you state. Another option is to lie to yourself and others by saying one thing and then doing something to the contrary.

This is not meant to judge you. My goal is for you to have a better idea of your true values because they are critical components of your decision-making lens. It is easy for you to say what you would do in a given situation. What you actually do in that situation is the real test. You really won't know until you live through it. As mentioned earlier, it is so easy to be the armchair quarterback. Talking a good game is much different than actually playing the game.

Another thing to consider is how to deal with competing or opposing values. Being honest may be one of your core values. However, it may be difficult to be honest all the time due to conflicting values. Here is a simple example that most people have faced in their lives.

Your spouse or co-worker comes in with a new hairstyle. They say, with an enthusiastic big smile on their face, "I just love my new cut, what do you think?" You hate it. Do you express your honest feelings or do you say it is great? Your competing value is you don't want your spouse/co-worker to have hurt feelings. You convincingly say, "I love the new cut." In this case you are a liar. You did not live up to your value of honesty. However, you did live up to your value of not hurting your spouse/co-worker. On the flip side, you could have told them your true feelings because you respect them enough to give them honest feedback regardless of how they feel about your comments.

As you can see, competing values can cause internal conflict. This harmless, well-meaning example, is just one of the many challenges you will be processing when making a decision. Unfortunately, some of the decisions we have to make with competing values have much greater consequences.

Since values play such an important role in the DMP it is important you know your values. The last thing you should be doing is reviewing your values if a quick decision needs to be made in extreme circumstances.

Emotions - Anger, happiness, sadness, love, hate, and fear are just a few of the emotions we can feel at any moment of the day. You know from your experience that your emotions have tremendous influence in your DMP. I am willing to bet you have made a decision, while being very angry, that you have regretted. If you were not angry you would likely have made a different decision in that same situation.

Since controlling intense emotions is difficult, it is important you at least acknowledge the fact that intense emotions can overpower the DMP. Recognizing a problem is the first step in correcting it. There are many techniques one can use to temper strong emotions. Rather than discuss them here I will address them in *Appendix 2.*

You will do almost anything for someone you love. You may feel you have absolutely no control over that feeling. If I could suggest ways to control that emotion I could make a fortune by writing another book on the subject. Love is such a powerful feeling it is hard to control. In fact, controlling love is so powerful I suggest you try avoiding situations where you may need to make critical decisions regarding loved ones that directly affect others.

The in-flight safety talk on a plane tells you to put on your oxygen mask before you put one on your child. Your love for your offspring may have you doing the opposite, which could cause you to black out and therefore be useless to your child. These guidelines were established, without emotion, to help protect you and your loved ones. In the long run these recommendations will be more effective in keeping both of you from suffering from lack of oxygen.

Non-emotional decisions tend to be more effective than intense emotional ones. The better you can deal with your emotions in critical situations the better for all involved. In reality, this is a lot easier said than done. You are not a robot so emotions are part of your lens. Emotions in their normal range can add soul and compassion into the DMP. Strong emotions will be discussed later in the **Lens Filter** section.

Drive - The intensity of energy you put into action is called drive. Strong drive due to urgency and/or passion can help you get things done as long as it isn't taken to extremes.

The most common problem I have seen with too much drive is pushing yourself or the group too hard. Minor and overuse injuries and/or undue fatigue from pushing too hard during the first day of a multi-day trip can cause lasting consequences throughout the remainder of the trip.

I once read there are three types of people: Those who watch things happen; those who make things happen; and those who wonder what happened? In such cases the one who makes things happen has the drive.

Ego - The best description I have for ego, with respect to the points I wish to make, is "self-image and self-worth." This is how you view and feel about yourself. We all have egos. The question is, does your ego inhibit or facilitate effective decisions? How big is your ego and, more importantly, are you aware of it? Is the image you have of yourself easily affected? How far will you push to prove to yourself that you've still got it? Do you have enough self-worth to not worry about your self-image? Do you have enough belief in yourself to make difficult decisions? Do you accept responsibilities for your mistakes or do you blame others? How you answer these questions can provide a window to your ego.

There is nothing wrong with self-interest. I strongly believe you need to take care of yourself if you want to effectively help others. However, if you make it all about you, then your ego can be negatively affecting your other lens-factors. Developing a strong, well-grounded, sense of self-worth is the best defense against too much concern for self-image and is the foundation of good self-confidence, which is necessary for making difficult decisions.

Reputation – I am making a specific distinction between your ego and your reputation. Your ego is how you see yourself. Your reputation is how the rest of the world views you and has no affect on your self-image or your self-worth unless you allow it. Peer pressure can only exist if you give a higher priority to how others view you over how you view yourself. If you give in to peer pressure you are putting yourself second.

Most peer pressure is self-imposed rather than overt. When working with adults I have rarely seen someone daring another in their group to do something risky. More commonly we are swayed because we believe the rest of our group will think less of us if we do not take the challenge. The part of your ego that counteracts peer pressure is your self-worth, which is saying you are good enough even if you don't do the activity. I always applaud the first member of the group who speaks up and says, "I am not comfortable with this situation." All of a sudden a few more speak up saying they too are not sure about accepting the risks involved.

A more subtle form of self-imposed peer pressure is our desire to belong. It is amazing what people are willing to do in order to be included, regardless of how it goes against their values.

Then there are the overt pressures of society and your peers to do things their way, which can affect your reputation if you do not comply. If your livelihood is dependent upon your guiding company, then concern for your reputation and that of your company are very important, which means it can be an important lens-factor. The key is to put that concern into a proper perspective when it involves the welfare of others.

You are a seasoned adventure guide. During a trip you decide to cancel the trip due to weather concerns. In your advertising you clearly state only partial refunds will be given if the trip is cancelled mid-way due to environmental factors. You are confident you made the right call due to your twenty years of experience and your concern for your client's safety. However, some in the group didn't think the weather was too bad and they are vocal about it to the point of saying you don't know what you are doing. At the end of the trip you tell the entire group you are sorry you aborted the trip but in your professional opinion, client welfare was more important than client disappointment. You add that you feel so strongly about your decision that you will be issuing full refunds.

This is an example of your ego believing in yourself while the comments of some could affect your reputation. Your concern for reputation did not trump your concern for your clients. However you are still concerned about your reputation and that of your business so you decided to issue full refunds. You are putting your money where your mouth is, with respect to your decision, which will likely enhance your reputation.

Desires - You have desires. You have hopes and dreams. Desires often fuel your drive. If you really want something, that desire will likely be the impetus to your drive. If you know your desires you can put them into perspective when making decisions.

When I directed Adventure Programs at U.C. Santa Barbara, it was important to me to have participants fill out course evaluations to help improve aspects of the program. Part of the evaluation was commenting on the instructor and/or the leaders. I have to say many of my college-age leaders were very disappointed with a less than stellar review. Some were devastated. I learned to keep a box of Kleenex on my desk for such events. It turned out that many of my leaders had a desire that everyone on the trip was going to like them and love the trip. Their desire for being liked, while being quite understandably normal, merely left them in a position for being disappointed. I would council them to change their desires to things that were more in their control. I would tell them the best you can do is provide the participant the opportunity to have a good time. Whether or not they chose to do so was up to them.

My concern as a program director was how far would my staff go in trying to provide a good time. Would they forego certain safety regulations because participants preferred not to follow them? Would they allow participants to remove a PFD (Personal Floatation Device) so they could get a better sun tan while paddling? Our program risk management guidelines require PFD's be worn when a participant is in a watercraft on the water. Would my leaders allow participants to drink alcohol or use recreational drugs even though we had a very explicit no drugs or alcohol policy required by the University? These examples show how one's desires can influence a decision in a negative way.

Regulations are a lens-factor, which will be discussed later, but are often an opposing factor to having a good time, which causes conflict in your lens. In the examples above I am stating the point of view of a program director that's responsible for enforcing regulations. Aside from the program liability, these regulations often err on the side of safety for the participant. If we combine the alcohol and the disregard for a PFD on a river trip, we are now entering the realm of being irresponsible, unsafe and negligent.

A common challenge we regularly face when making decisions is *want* versus *need*. Our most basic *needs* are maintaining body temperature, staying hydrated, getting nourishment, having shelter and feeling secure, which are physiological and psychological needs.

Wants can be an endless list. Most of the purchases in our current consumer society are based on wants rather than real needs. Desire is something you want but it may not be needed. How many extra items do you pack in your backpack that you want but you really don't need? Needs are usually fairly simple. Wants tend to complicate matters. It is important for you to be able to recognize the difference between the two. Your *needs* should take priority over your *wants*.

Others - You do not live in a vacuum. Most, if not all, of your decisions will have an affect on others and your environment. Concern for others may already be part of your beliefs, values, desires, and some other lens-factors. In case it isn't, I have included it as a separate factor. How you prioritize your needs against the needs of others can be difficult depending on the situation. There is a value that Star Trek's Spock references, which I pose to you in two questions. Do the needs of many outweigh the needs of the few or the one? Do the needs of the few or the one outweigh the needs of the many? If you consider these questions in your DMP then thinking of others is one of your chosen lens-factors.

If you are a guide, addressing the needs of others is not only necessary and/or required; it must be a high priority in any of your decisions. If you are not going to consider others then you have no business being a guide.

I also include the environment when I say others. What impact do your decisions have on your surroundings, which is all of Mother Nature?

Expectations - When you feel something is promised to you there is some belief that your expectation will be met. Just suggesting something may trigger expectations. Expectations are different from desires. If you want something, it is a desire. If someone promises you something you will most likely expect it to occur, which is a potential pitfall for organized trips.

If your advertised itinerary is forcing you to meet the expectations of your participants you could be putting your group in harms way if weather conditions are slowing your anticipated pace. Do you push the group to get to the planned destination or do you adjust to the conditions and not fulfill expectations? The expectations forcing your decisions could be not only of the group, but yours as well.

One of the best ways in dealing with the above example is learning how to set expectations. As soon as you describe your trip in your marketing/promotional materials you are planting the seeds of expectations. Therefore it is important to choose your advertising words carefully. Since you never know what Mother Nature will throw at you on the trip, clearly state that all itineraries are flexible due to weather conditions and the collective nature of the group. Reiterate that point whenever a participant asks if they will see or do something specific. My standard reply is, "If the environment and the group performance goes as anticipated we will try to get it done." I was surprised how a simple question could set expectations.

During my first year of running Adventure Programs I asked participants during our pre-trip meeting, "What would you like to have for breakfast and dinner for the planned 3 day-2 night trip?" At the end of the trip there were always comments about the food on the post-trip evaluations. I eventually realized I was in a no-win situation when I asked them what they wanted. There are 12 participants + two leaders on a typical group trip. There are a total of two dinners and three breakfasts during the trip. If all 12 asked for something different for dinner, at most I would be satisfying only two out of 12, which means I met the expectations of 16% of the group, not including the leaders - not good odds for satisfying expectations. The second year I no longer asked what the group wanted for meals. I only asked their dietary restrictions. The post-trip evaluations rarely ever mentioned food again, nor have they since.

Learning how to, or not to, set expectations became an important aspect of running the program. More importantly, I made it clear to the staff that the well-being of the participants and the staff was their top priority while meeting expectations was ranked much lower.

It is important to realize that everyone who comes on an organized trip has a list of expectations, aside from the expectations you try to set in your advertising. Most of the time, you will never know what those expectations are because they will be unsaid. With that in mind, I have found it very beneficial to ask, during the group introduction circle, what participants expected while on the trip. If I know an expectation cannot be met, I would inform the participant up front rather than have them anticipating for the entire trip only to be disappointed at the end. I have found that knowing at the beginning of the trip, even though they are still disappointed, allowed them to focus on other aspects of the trip and they leave the trip with a better feeling.

My greater concern is our self-imposed expectations, which oftentimes dictate our behavior. These expectations can become self-imposed pressures if we are not careful.

I recently shared a room with Jim at a Paddlesports show. The topic of routines came up and he said if he starts his day late he feels like he is behind all day long. I asked him if he puts in the same number of hours regardless of his starting time. He said yes. I immediately asked, "If you are going to put in eight hours, regardless of your start time, why do you feel behind?" He said, "I just do." He also added it made him feel rushed and it was more stressful. We then had a great discussion about the self-imposed pressures as a result our own expectations.

I know some of my self-imposed expectations are a result of the values my father tried to instill in me. I am not a perfectionist, but I am close to being one. "If you are going to do a job, do it well or don't do it at all" is what my dad drilled into my head. I freely admit I can go overboard but I am aware of it now. Not so in my early years, which caused undue pressure when doing projects. I am sure most of us have our parent's voices in our heads at the root of many of our expectations. If you have these self-imposed expectations that can negatively affect your performance and/or health, it is time to make some adjustments. What is even more important is being aware of them. In Jim's case, his feeling of being behind can drive him or rush him. Either of these - in excess - does not usually lead to one's best performance.

Preferences - Preference is defined as "to like better or give priority." Preferences are the decisions you have already made regarding one thing versus another. I prefer vanilla ice cream to chocolate ice cream. I prefer synthetic garments to wool garments. You have already chosen which items you prefer. Knowing your preferences can save time in decision-making.

Acknowledging your preferences does not mean you have to choose your preferred item all the time. It is OK to mix it up once in a while. However, knowing you prefer the freeze-dried beef stroganoff meal for camping can make shopping a little quicker.

As a program director I had to make regular equipment purchases. I can tell you I had definite preferences as to which companies I used and which equipment I purchased. Function, longevity, guarantees and price were the main criteria used when deciding my preferences. It can be very time consuming to research all companies and equipment possibilities each time you need to make a purchase. I would stick with my preferred suppliers and change if I came across something better. Again my preferences allowed me to be more efficient time wise when getting equipment.

It is normal to have preferences and it is important that you know what they are. If you are leading others, knowing their preferences can be very helpful in running a smooth trip.

Awareness - Your level of awareness is a critical factor in your lens. Awareness of your surroundings, of others and especially yourself (your lens) is how you gather information. The greater your awareness, the more information you have for your decision. Keep in mind that all of the information you gather may not be relevant. How you focus your lens, your experience and other factors will influence relevancy. However, if you are not aware of important information it may negatively affect your decision.

As an outdoor professional I have learned to constantly scan my surroundings. My head is moving and my senses are on constant alert as to any changes. Whenever possible, I position myself to see as many of the clients in my charge during an outing. I am checking in with them regularly to hear what they have to say. I am also checking in with myself because I know if I am not at 100% it can and will affect my performance. If I cannot be an asset to the group - I should not be leading them.

Just because you are aware does not mean you will gather the necessary and appropriate information. As I mentioned earlier, you may not even know what to look for while scanning or not recognize it. Your experiences will increase your awareness if you learn from them. Also the more you know, the more information you can gather.

The key to effective awareness is being able to recognize what is relevant and knowing what isn't. Being able to distinguish between the two is learned through experience.

Experience - Experience is the practical knowledge and skills you have learned through observation and participation in events. My dad was a big fan of the ***School of Hard Knocks***. "What I hear I forget; what I see I remember; and what I do I know!" is a saying that I have kept in mind when I train others to be leaders. Having the trainee's actually perform it is much better than just talking about what to do. My ambulance ride-along and ER hours during my EMT training made all the reading and lectures pale by comparison. Having to perform CPR on more than one occasion changed the way I taught CPR to my students.

It is said, "Good judgment is learned from experience and experience is learned from bad judgment." This quote implies we learn from our mistakes. If we try something and it doesn't work, we usually wonder why and probably won't do the same thing again given the same situation. Therefore, we learn from not getting the results we wanted.

Not learning from your ineffective decisions brings to mind the Chinese definition of insanity: "Repeating the same action expecting a different result." Another quote that I enjoy is, "Fool me once, shame on you; fool me twice, shame on me." Hopefully you learn from your mistakes, which is part of your experience.

While driving cross-country to grad school in Oregon I encountered a weather phenomenon I had never seen before. I was in one of the plains states traveling the interstate. The dark skies ahead told me a storm was approaching. The rain had not started - not even a drop on the windshield. Then I saw what appeared to be a haze. Suddenly a downpour consumed me. The haze was a curtain of rain, so heavy I could barely see beyond the front end of the car. It was as if I had driven right into a waterfall.

Over twenty years later, while leading a staff-training trip on the Colorado River below Lake Mead, I saw this same type of haze advancing towards our group. The trainees were told to keep their rain gear easily accessible due to the weather forecast and the overhead clouds. As soon as I saw the haze I started to don my paddle jacket. I signaled to the group and pointed to the haze. They just sat there until the wall of water was upon them. Then they scrambled to get their rain gear on. Those who buried their gear learned a great lesson. I too would have been caught off guard had not that haze been part of my experience.

As I was donning my paddle jacket I noticed my two senior staff that were running the trip with me had also put on rain gear. Later I asked them if they, too, had recognized that phenomenon? They said "No" so I asked why they did put on their rain gear at that moment. They replied, "If you were putting on your gear we thought we better do it too." I appreciated the fact they were paying attention. I felt flattered I had been a role model in that instance.

Here is a thought for your consideration. How much do you learn from your successes or perceived successes? It is common to think you took the correct actions because you got the expected result. However, there may be an occasion where your actions did not really produce the result but other circumstances did. When you get your expected result, it may be worth doing a quick review to see if it was indeed the result of your actions rather than other factors. Perhaps next time those same actions may not get the same result.

As an example, let's look at bear proofing your food while backpacking. Years ago, before bear-proof canisters, we had to hang our food. I am sure many folks still do if it is permitted in your area. You read how to do it and you follow the recommended guidelines for hanging your food. Success! You wake up each morning and your food is still there. In fact, after the next ten outings you feel like a bear-proof expert. Then on trip eleven you wake up to find your food gone. Was your technique really that successful or were your first ten outings never tested because no bears came by the camp?

The high percentage of the time (I cannot say all the time) your actions will be the reason you get your expected result. When you don't get your expected result you will review what you did. I am just asking you to also review your actions when you are successful. Perhaps ask yourself "Even though it worked could I have done it differently or better?"

The key to learning from your experiences is through reflecting on the results of your actions. I am saddened and concerned at the lack of reflection time in this faster, electronic, ever-connected world we live in. Each night during the trip I reflect upon my day and my actions. I do it again at the end of the trip. I have found writing in journals to be a great tool for reflection, learning and solidifying my experiences. One of my journal questions is, "What did I learn from this trip?"

Using the experiences of others can be an effective way to improve your lens. Even though you may not have lived the experience, reading what others have done gives you more information for your lens. I love reading about the mishaps of others to expand my collective knowledge. Imagining and/or acting out the mishaps of others in role-playing scenarios are great ways to reinforce "what to do and what not to do."

Knowledge - Everything you have learned in your life is your collective knowledge. It is the information you have gathered to date that is stored in your brain. The more knowledge you amass, the more information you will have at your disposal when making a decision. If you are going into a new area, the more you learn about that area, the more information you will have when it comes time to making a decision. Gathering "local knowledge" is invaluable when exploring new areas.

You will never know everything, because there is just too much information. However, you will be well rewarded if you learn as much as you can about the environments you will be entering during your adventures.

Personally I believe one of the most important areas of study for any outdoors person is first aid. You can never learn too much first aid. It can help you save a life, minimize an injury, prevent an injury and provide possible peace of mind after an emergency - because you were prepared.

It is said, "A little bit of knowledge is a dangerous thing." I think all knowledge is beneficial. The important thing is what you do with that little bit. If you think you now know it all then you will probably be a disaster waiting to happen. When it comes to learning I believe enough is *never* enough.

Skills - I define skills as physical knowledge versus our intellectual knowledge that I just discussed. Skills are coordinated actions. You use your body in a particular way to make things happen. What I hear I forget (if you remember it is part of your intellectual knowledge). What I see I remember is intellectual knowledge. What I do, I know, is learning the skills. Making decisions and taking actions are skills, which can be improved through practice and repetition.

Skills need to be used regularly or they tend to get rusty. "Use it or lose it" is a wise and accurate saying. I ask my students, "When do you know your skills no longer work?" Unfortunately for many, it is when they need the skill and they can no longer do it. Just because your brain remembers how to do it, does not mean your body can still perform it. It is a good idea to practice the skills you anticipate you will need for your adventure. It's not only reassuring; it is the only way to prove your skills are still reliable. This message has been approved by Wayne's voice of experience!

Rolling a kayak is an example of a skill that can slip away from you quickly if not practiced regularly. Yet I know many kayakers who say if their roll doesn't work they will do their paddle float recovery. However, is that paddle float recovery still reliable? Many paddlers learned the paddle float recovery in their basic class and have never used it again. Unfortunately I had a former student/friend who was found dead outside his boat due to exposure, because he did not get back into his kayak. The last time I saw him attempt his solo recovery I told him he should not be going out alone until he improves his performance because his self-recovery skills did not look reliable.

22

Again, you do not want to find out your skills are no longer viable when you need them, especially if your well-being depends on it.

Commitments - A commitment is an agreement or a pledge to do something in the future. When you commit to taking an action in the future it can radically affect your lens and how you view and consider your possible options.

The major commitments in people's lives are to loved ones, family, friends, promises, spiritual beliefs, work and school. Work and school commitments usually keep you on a tight schedule. If you let it, these time commitments can cause you to get into difficult situations because you feel you need to get home in time to go to work or school. If you are in a wilderness area and need to get out today because of work tomorrow, you could be putting yourself at greater risk if the weather conditions suggest you stay put for another day. This is when your commitment may be negatively affecting your lens. The question that should be asked in this situation is, "If I did not have to go to work or school tomorrow would I stay put because of the weather?" I have yet to see a tombstone inscribed with, "I wish I spent more time at work."

On the opposite side, a busy work or school schedule leaves you with limited recreation time. How many people get off work on Friday night and jump in their car to get to the ski lodge that same night to make the most of their weekend even if it's a four to six hour drive? I know I am certainly not at my best after a full day's work with an additional long drive at night most likely on snowy or icy roads in the dark. I once read more injuries and incidents occur getting to and from your adventure than on the outing itself. I had a friend who was killed in India while riding in a cab on his way to the river for a first descent. We thought the river was the dangerous part of the trip.

With limited time, commitments can make rushing to and from adventures inevitable. I am not saying not to do it. I have done it on too many occasions throughout my life as well. I am asking you to keep a reasonable perspective in how much you push your schedule.

Your commitment to your family and friends can be very powerful. Because I consider close friends as the family that I have chosen, I know I would risk my life for them. At that level of commitment, devotion will certainly affect my decisions.

If you have a specific itinerary set for your trip you may end up forcing decisions based upon that schedule. An itinerary is a form of commitment. Another form of commitment is promises made to participants as part of the trip. (i.e. wildlife viewing, hiking locations, hot springs, freshly caught fish, etc...). If you push too hard to make these commitments happen you may be compromising the well-being of the group. If you push the group in order to get to the hot springs you could be causing overuse injuries due to your need to fulfill the commitment of reaching that specific destination.

Planning is necessary. However, your plans need to be flexible. One of the common mistakes made by outdoor enthusiasts is sticking to the itinerary rather than adjusting their itinerary to meet the needs of the environment and/or those involved. There is nothing wrong with commitments or making plans as long as you allow flexibility.

    Regulations – Regulations include laws, rules you obey, policies, or any set of guidelines you have committed to or are required to follow. You either choose to follow regulations or you do not. If you are not concerned about the consequences of ignoring regulations then regulations really don't matter. If, however, you believe in following regulations or have committed to do so, then the regulations will be an important factor in your lens. You may have a preference to do Plan A, but regulations you have chosen to obey do not allow it so you opt for Plan B instead.

The sign on the trail clearly states, "Do not cut switchbacks."
You are in a hurry to get back to trailhead and you see it
would be a lot quicker to go straight down and cut the
switchbacks. The steepness doesn't bother you and you see
that others have done the same thing so you go for it. There
are no rangers around so who cares? You have ignored a
policy that helps maintain the quality of the trail. When the
rains come and the snow melts these cross cuts, created by you
and the other inconsiderate (@^&@#%) hikers, erode the
trail. In some cases trails have been ruined. It also adds to the
work and cost of maintaining trails for all to enjoy. This is just
one example of some possible consequences when regulations
are not followed.

Are there times when regulations need to be ignored?
Possibly yes, in a life or death situation perhaps, but there
still may be consequences. Rather than giving a serious dire
example I will attempt a little environmental humor.

The man stands before the judge because he killed and ate a
California condor, a bird on the endangered species list. He
claimed he was lost in the wilderness and needed to do it to
survive. The man added that he had tremendous respect for
the environment and felt he had no other choice. The judge
took the man's reasoning into consideration and did not
punish him. The judge, being curious, asked the man what
condor tasted like? The man replied it was a cross between a
bald eagle and a spotted owl.

Physical status – I am defining physical status as your
overall physical capabilities with respect to strength,
coordination, agility, fitness and endurance. Some examples
are your hiking pace, stamina and/or the weight you can
carry. It is what you can physically do with respect to your
body.

It is important to know your body's limitations and
capabilities. Knowing your hiking pace with a full pack
versus hiking with a daypack is essential when calculating
your hiking distance for a given day. Knowing how much you

can carry will determine what you bring as well as how long you can stay out before needing to resupply. Knowing how often your body needs to be fueled and hydrated is important. Let's face it; we need our body to execute the decisions we make.

In March of 2015 I stopped at the Grand Canyon as I circumnavigated the contiguous US teaching kayaking clinics. I felt like doing an ambitious day hike from the South Rim. I decided to hike down to the Colorado River on the south Kiabab trail and back up to the rim via the Bright Angel trail in one day. It turned out to be a 16.1 mile hike with a combined elevation loss/gain of 10,000 feet. I had done the hike 30 years earlier and thought I could still do it even though my 65th birthday was just three months away. I can honestly say I over estimated my physical status. I completed the hike - but the last three miles was on sheer willpower alone. My energy stores were completely depleted. If I hadn't had my hiking poles along I would not have made it. Needless to say, a lot of Aleve was consumed in the days to follow. Even though I completed the hike, there were painful consequences because my assessment of my physical status was based more upon memory rather than recent performance.

Physiological status – Physiology is the study of our body's functions: our circulation; respiration; internal temperature; nervous system; muscles; bones and metabolism, etc... Our body is a complex living organism and we need to: maintain body temperature; nourish it; stay well hydrated; give it rest and sleep to function at reasonable levels – and we need to excrete waste products from it.

You can be in the peak of fitness (your physical status) but a case of food poisoning in the back country can curl you up into a painful ball praying for death. Anyone who has gotten severely seasick knows how debilitating and retching that ordeal can be. The only thing you can do is to lie there and be sick.

There are also those times when normal body functions take priority. When you have to "go" nothing else matters. If time permits, take care of business first and then make your decision. I regularly tell my clients, "If nature calls, answer."

Since the greatest cause of death in the outdoors is due to exposure to the elements, maintaining normal body temperature and staying hydrated need to be a priority, not only for survival, but also for clear thinking.

Psychological status – Our behavior is affected by how our brain works. There is a range of behavior that is considered normal. "Abnormal" behavior is a topic onto itself and beyond the scope of this discussion.

How well you are adjusted to your issues is important when making decisions. As an example, fear is a self-preservation emotion that gives us pause before proceeding. A phobia is an extreme fear (beyond the normal range) that can paralyze you, which definitely affects your decision-making ability no matter what logic dictates.

Psychological issues are very personal and how you deal with those issues is up to you. It is important to understand how your personal issues can affect your decision-making process.

If you have a phobia regarding grizzly bears, then it would not be wise to allow yourself to be in areas where grizzlies are present. If your response to seeing a bear is to run for the hills you could cause the bear to chase you. Grizzly Bear protocol says **not** to run when first seeing the bear. If you cannot control reactions due to certain psychological issues then you need to avoid the situations or learn how to overcome those issues before getting into them in the first place.

Other behavioral issues worth mentioning besides fear include rage, revenge, obsession and violence. These are extreme behaviors, which can drastically affect your decision-making process. These extreme feelings can be blinding and we will address them further in the **Lens Filter** section of this chapter.

   Risk assessment - Risk is in the eye of the beholder. Each of us has our own view of what is an acceptable level of risk and what is not. It is important you have an understanding of your own personal risk assessment and risk philosophy, especially if you are making decisions that include others.

Do you have good risk assessment skills or are you oblivious to the possible risks in outdoor environments or outdoor activities? Do you like to live on the edge or are you very cautious? Part of making a decision includes assessing risk. Your acceptable level of risk may be very different from those in your group. If so, do you even take that into consideration when making a decision that could affect others as well? I have learned from experience that our assessment and willingness to take risks can change instantly if our physical and emotional state changes.

One day when kayaking the upper Merced River in California I saw one of my friends get worked over after going over a waterfall. He was held in a keeper hole at the bottom of the falls. His kayak was flipping end over end for quite a while. Despite being an excellent boater he just couldn't paddle out of that hole. He eventually swam out and we retrieved him and his kayak.

After resting on the shore for a while we asked if he was ready to continue. I was very impressed with his answer. He freely admitted his confidence was shot for the day and we should continue without him. With respect to risk, the assessment of the river had not changed. However, his willingness to take the risks had changed due to his recent experience. He knew himself well enough and chose not continue for the day. His skills had not changed, but his confidence in his skills at that moment had changed. Again, I admired his personal assessment and even more his willingness to reveal it to his peers. His reputation (previously discussed lens-factor) was not a consideration in his decision-making lens.

I have devoted an entire chapter to risk assessment later in the book. In that chapter you will find a risk assessment questionnaire that may help you clarify your views on risk.

Time – Time is fleeting. It is constantly ticking by as we go through our DMP, so it is often an important lens-factor. You cannot stop it, but you can learn how to use it wisely. Time management is an invaluable skill to hone. I always carry a watch on every adventure. Effective planning and knowing when to take action is dependent on proper timing. In addition, some medical emergencies need accurate time data, which requires a timepiece.

Money - One would think that money should not be a consideration during adventures. When you are in the outdoors, money is not usually going to help you very much unless you want to use the paper bills as kindling for a fire. Seriously, having some emergency cash is always a good idea when on a trip.

I raise the issue of money because it is very much a concern prior to your adventure. I have seen lots of inadequate equipment due to individuals trying to save a buck. Poor sleeping bags, leaking raincoats and bad footwear are at the top of the list. Most of us have limited resources. I am not concerned about the brand name. I believe your equipment purchases should be functional and reliable. Quality equipment keeps an adventure enjoyable. Keep that in mind when using your DMP when purchasing equipment.

I have also seen novices get into trouble because they were untrained. Rather than paying for a training class, they figure they can do it on their own. Since I am an avid "Do it yourself (DIY)" individual, I am not against DIY. However, there are many outdoor sports that require some basic training at the very least. All I can say is, "Pay now or pay later."

Future hindsight – I define hindsight as "shoulding" all over yourself. I should have done this or done that. Actual hindsight can only occur if you have already taken the action and you are looking back at the results.

Future hindsight is to put yourself into the future in order to look back on your planned actions. The question I ask myself in my DMP is, "How am I going to feel about this decision in one day, one week, one month or years from now?" That question has helped me many times in my life and many others who have learned from my advice.

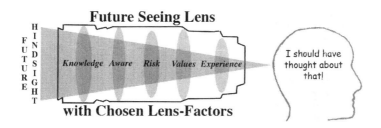

In 1991 I was on a long flight from Los Angeles to the United Kingdom along with my fellow teammates on the US Surf Kayaking Team heading to the World Championships in Thurso Scotland, located on the northern tip of the UK. We were going to be in the UK for a month, which gave us sightseeing time aside from competing. All of us were focused on the upcoming competition. That tunnel vision did not include sightseeing. However I decided to look ahead and ask, "When I am back home am I going say I wish I would have seen this or wish I had done that?" With that in mind I decided to make a list of the top things I wanted to do in the UK if time allowed. I went to my teammates and suggested they do the same and to prioritize their wishes. After we all made our lists I had them all agree that we will make sure everyone got their number one wish fulfilled and then we would try to meet the number twos and threes.

After compiling the list we worked the driving route to make these happen. Some of our desires were the same, which made planning a little easier. It also allowed us to participate in *some events that we never thought of. In this case looking ahead, to look back, made our experience much more rewarding. For the record, my number one priority was rolling my kayak in Loch Ness. The rest of the gang joined in. Unfortunately, Dan Crandall lost his brand new sunglasses in the lake. I recently heard, that the last time Nessie was seen she was sporting some new shades.*

In reality, hindsight is your own evaluation (judgment) of the decisions you have made. I am asking you to look ahead to look back and try to anticipate how you are going to feel regarding what you are about to do or planning to do.

Gut feeling - Sometimes there is no tangible reason for you to do something except for a feeling in your gut. My gut feeling usually speaks up when I am ready to choose my action. My DMP up to the point of acting says, "This is the best thing to do." However, my gut feeling tells me I should not do it. My gut doesn't tell me why I shouldn't do it; the gut just sends nasty little doubts to my brain.

Even though my gut feeling has never been 100% accurate, it has been correct more times than not, which forces me to pause and possibly re-evaluate. You will have to decide how much you should listen to your gut feelings. While gut feelings are real, even if they are not tangible, how you prioritize them will be part of your process.

I believe, the better you understand the factors in your lens and use those factors in a rational, unemotional state of mind, the less often your gut is going to be speaking to you.

Before each multi-day trip I would meet with the two trip leaders to review the trip. During that meeting I would tell them, "If you feel the need to end the trip early or make radical changes to the trip it will be your call, even if it were a gut feeling." Of course we will be discussing the reasons for the decision in a post-trip meeting, but I would rather give a refund than hear a leader say, after the fact, "I had a gut feeling something was going to happen."

When anyone has feelings of doom it usually affects their perceptions and their decision-making. If this gut feeling is distracting one of my trip leaders they are probably not functioning at their best and they should probably cancel the trip.

As mentioned at the beginning of this chapter, you may have other factors that make up your lens. I have included the ones that I have used during my years as an adventure educator. Regardless of the number of factors in your lens, the important point is how well you use and know your lens. Knowing your lens truly means knowing yourself.

Focusing Your Lens
Now that we have listed and explained many different factors that can be used for making decisions it is time to discuss how to manage them. Earlier I compared our decision-making lens to a camera lens. Continuing with that analogy let's discuss focusing your lens. In photography you have many different lenses from which to choose: wide angle; telephoto; macro and normal range to name a few. Each of these specialty lenses is used to view the world in a particular way due to the specific optics that are chosen and then placed in the appropriate order.

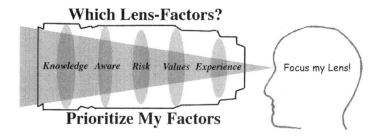

Rather than confusing your DMP with multiple lenses I want you to think of your decision-making lens as just one big lens that you use for all of your decisions. What makes your one lens so versatile is it has the ability to use any or all of your lens-factors in whatever priority order you wish. This gives your lens almost infinite possibilities. The other great thing about your decision-making lens is the choosing and prioritizing process can be done in an instant. The more you are in touch with your different lens-factors the easier it will be for you to focus your lens.

Before I continue I want to be clear in what I mean when I discuss prioritizing your lens-factors. It refers to the importance, the weight, of each factor. If you pick five lens-factors all with the same priority then all of those factors will be considered equally in your decision. However, if you give one a greater weight over another then that factor will be more important in your decision, which means it has higher priority.

In a camera lens you turn the outside of the lens to adjust the internal optics to focus the lens. In decision-making you focus your lens by picking and prioritizing which factors you will be using for the event in question. The lens-factors you engage for one decision may likely be different from the ones you choose for another decision. In addition, by changing the priority of the chosen factors you may get a different result even though you are using the same factors.

As an example, if I have to choose which jacket to take on a day hike, the factors I will be using in my lens (in priority order) are:
• Staying warm (Desire & Experience)
• The forecasted conditions (Expectations)
• Wearing a blue jacket instead of another color (Preference)

The lens for this decision had four of the twenty-four listed lens-factors in this order of priority. Keeping warm was my highest concern. Then I found the jacket that met that need (through experience) along with addressing the other two chosen factors. I chose my mid-weight blue jacket.

If I changed the priority of these factors and put color as my top priority and keeping warm as a lower priority, I may have picked a different one of my five blue jackets that may not be as warm. How you prioritize your factors is just as important as deciding which ones to choose. Some decisions may only need a few lens-factors, while others may necessitate many others.

As you will see in the next chapter there are six major steps in the DMP. Each different step may necessitate adjusting your lens-factors (refocusing your lens). You will be choosing and prioritizing the factors you believe to be necessary for each step of the process. To be clear, when I refer to your lens I am referring to the factors you have chosen and how you prioritized them.

With so many factors comprising your lens learning how to focus is going to take time. You will not have time nor do you need to review all of the factors in your lens for every decision. Instead, you will be selecting and prioritizing the lens-factors you feel are appropriate for each situation. If, after the decision, you realize you should or shouldn't have engaged certain factors you can adjust your lens the next time in a similar circumstance. Earlier we defined lens as a manner at which you view something. Therefore how you focus your lens will determine how you see and respond.

If you are like most people, all of the factors on your list are not weighted equally. There are some, your values for example, that may regularly dominate most, if not all of your decisions. The weight and the priority of your factors will, and I believe should, vary to meet the needs of the event.

The greatest difficulty for me comes when I have opposition and/or competition among and within my lens-factors. Having to choose one value over another is never easy. Deciding between two intense desires is also difficult. It is easier for me to focus when my chosen factors are in unison.

In my pre-trip meetings with my staff I would remind them of what their priorities should be with respect to program expectations when making decisions. Number one was to bring everyone back alive and in one piece. If everyone is

34

doing well, then number two was trying to provide what we promised in our advertising. The third was dealing with program responsibilities (equipment, vehicles, reports and finances) if numbers one and two were going well. My goal was to prompt them to focus their lens on the well-being of the participants.

As you learn to focus your lens, be careful not to limit yourself. In photography there are zoom lenses that are designed to see a small area in the distance, but in so doing miss the big picture. Conversely, a wide-angle lens goes for the big picture while smaller items tend get lost within the larger view. A macro-lens is used for extreme close-ups. Since I am suggesting we think of one lens, we need to be careful of focusing too narrow or too wide. Sometimes you will miss things because of tunnel vision and other times have too much information to sort because you couldn't decide what was relevant. Focusing your lens effectively takes practice. You will make errors. Your successes and mistakes will help you hone your ability to focus more effectively.

Lens Filters
In photography lens filters are used to change everything seen by the lens. If you put an orange filter over a lens it affects all of the optics in the lens and the image will be tinted orange. While making a decision, if you put a filter over your lens it will affect all of your chosen lens-factors for each step of the DMP.

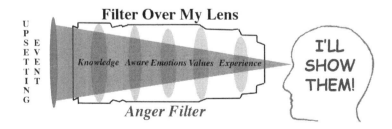

35

In my experience, a filter is usually one factor, taken to an extreme, which is being placed over your lens. Emotion is a factor in your lens. Let's say an event has made you angry. As you use your lens hopefully other factors will also be working that will put that anger into a lower priority in your lens. You still make an effective decision, while feeling anger, because you used other lens-factors in your decision. However, if anger is all you are thinking about then it becomes a filter, which influences all the factors being used in your lens. You may even end up using that filter for every step of the DMP.

Strong emotions easily become filters because many times they are hard to control. The same can be said for many of your lens-factors. Have you ever been wrong, but not admit it due to your ego? Ever purchase something because of the way it looked even though it didn't really fit or function well? What about enforcing a rule you know is bad or wrong? These are examples of filters in action.

There is a difference between prioritizing your lens-factors and a factor becoming a filter. Sometimes the distinction is obvious and other times it may be imperceptible. I wish I could sit here and tell you how to tell the difference. You will learn after you have made your decisions while reviewing the results. The important point is you recognize it and keep it in mind in the future.

Filters are not always bad. They can be useful when we need to put our entire focus on one factor. However, I think they are usually a disservice because any serious effective decision is rarely based on one factor. Here is a non-threatening example of a filter in action.

When I give my lecture on practicing good judgment I ask the participants to take a quick moment to scan the room and find all of the red items in that room. Then I ask them to close their eyes and point to those items and tell me what and where they are. Then I ask them, with their eyes still closed, to locate the green items? Most if not all in the room cannot point to the *green objects. The ones who cannot are using a red filter. Those who can, made **looking for red** a high priority factor in their lens, but their lens is still using other factors that allow them to see other colors.*

This simple example of a filter is literally making you see red. In this case red awareness was the filter, because you were only looking for one thing, which was the one color. It didn't matter what messages you were getting from your other lens-factors, because you let the filter control the input. Let's change the circumstances and possible consequences of this example.

Now you are looking for any trace of the green jacket your friend was wearing when he got caught in an avalanche. The debris field is also littered with numerous branches from pine trees so there is a lot of green causing you to focus on green even more. All you can think about is finding any trace of your friend's green parka, essentially putting the green filter over your lens while you search. Since you have chosen to think of nothing else, you run the risk of becoming a victim yourself to another avalanche since your green filter obscured your other lens-factors. You also may miss his brown pant leg if it were sticking out of the snow. Your lens will serve you better if you made looking for green a high priority lens-factor, instead of making it a filter, so other factors in your lens can be utilized such as monitoring the environment for additional slides, other colors or other clues, not to mention your own status in this cold and precarious environment.

One of the reasons we are terrible at proofreading what we have written is we know what we wrote and we expect to see it. In this example our expectations become a filter. One of the ways I proofread my spelling, which minimizes my expectations, is to read the words backwards. This way I see the words that are there, not what I think is there.

Before we leave the concept of filters I want to leave you with this example, I'm sure we can all relate to. "Does anything else matter when you are on the verge of peeing in your pants?" I ask this with a smile on my face.

As we move into describing the DMP think about your own lens-factors, which can make understanding the process more relevant. I hope you made your own list as you read mine. If not, it could be a good exercise for you to write down your list of lens-factors now before you continue to the next chapter. Use the blank pages at the end of the book to write down your list of lens-factors.

In addition, try to recall times when filters have caused you to make what you now view as poor decisions. Perhaps you have a particular filter that reoccurs too often. Before you can correct a problem you first need to identify it.

It all depends on your point of view.

CHAPTER 3

DECISION-MAKING PROCESS
REACTIVE DECISIONS

In order for a decision to be made there needs to be an **Event** that requires a decision. After we recognize the event, we need to **Evaluate** it. Once the event is evaluated we need to know our **Goals** with respect to making our decision. After identifying our goals we identify and consider the **Options** we believe will lead us to our goals. From those options we pick the one we think best and **Act** on it. After we take action we monitor our **Results** to see if we are achieving our goal. If not, we start the process over again.

There are two main categories in the decision-making process (DMP): reactive decisions and proactive decisions. The steps in the process are the same for both. This chapter will detail the steps of the DMP when <u>reacting</u> to an event.

Decision-Making Process Steps (EEGOAR):

Event	(Is happening or has happened)
Evaluate	(Gather relevant input & prioritize)
Goals	(Know desired outcome)
Options	(List possible viable options)
Action	(Choose your best option & act on it)
Results	(Getting desired outcome - adjust as needed)

To help define the steps of the DMP, I will use the following *Clear Lake Scenario* (*CLS*) as an example of a reactive decision.

After briefly speaking with the National Park ranger about different day hikes near my current location the Clear Lake trailhead was the closest. At the beginning of my solo hike I came to a fork in the trail with a sign showing two trails to Clear Lake. Trail 1 says 8.5 miles to the lake. Trail 2 says 5.0 miles to the lake. What is my course of action?

As I go through my steps of the DMP with respect to the Clear Lake hike, write down what you would do as a comparison.

Remember, there is no right or wrong. This exercise is meant for you to identify your lens-factors and to practice focusing your decision-making lens.

Within my responses I will be identifying the factors I have chosen for my lens (highlighted in **bold** letters) for each step of the DMP. Refer back to the Decision-Making Lens chapter for descriptions of the factors.

Event
What is an Event? For the purposes of this book we will define an event as a situation that may occur, is occurring or has occurred and you feel it needs to be addressed or you have a responsibility to address it. Reactive decisions are ones that respond to events that are happening and ones that have happened, but may require action now. If an event will or may happen in the future I will discuss it later in proactive decisions.

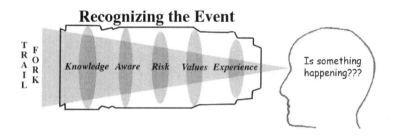

Recognizing the Event

Recognizing an event
Before you can decide if you need to make a decision regarding the event you need to realize there is an event. What if you were looking at the eagle flying above and you missed the fork and the trail sign? Due to being distracted you missed the fork in the trail, which would have meant making a decision. Being able to recognize and/or isolate an

40

event is an important factor. Being distracted is only one reason you can miss an event. Some others include:

- Distraction (as just mentioned);
- You were looking for something else;
- Just didn't notice (just not paying attention);
- Did not recognize it (poison oak without the leaves);
- Never encountered it before (completely new event);
- It was hidden (snake blending into the scenery);
- Your senses didn't catch it (didn't hear the rattlesnake due to other noise);
- You were not emotionally present (thinking of your break-up);
- Ignorance (never learned about it).

Multiple events

Even though we have been defining, identifying and describing a single event, there are times this one event can cause an immediate chain of events. Sometimes two or more things happen at once. The outdoors is a dynamic environment, so it is not uncommon to have multiple incidents to deal with at the same time.

These multiple events may each need its own decision or one decision may be necessary to deal with all of them. Regardless of how many events occur at the same time, you will need to follow the DMP for each one. Just like juggling balls, you need to keep an eye on each one. Evaluating the events (step 2) includes triage, which is prioritizing these multiple events.

If it begins raining on you when you come to the fork in the trail you need to decide what to do about the rain and still which trail to take. This is an example of two events where one of the events most likely affects your decision on the other event.

Events vs. conditions

This can be a bit confusing and even arbitrary depending on how you look at it. I define an event as an occurrence. I see conditions as the factors that are present around you when an event is about to happen, is happening or has happened. These conditions are occurring but you have already been dealing with them. If an event occurs while it is raining we will assume you are already dealing with the rain so the rain is an existing condition. However, if it is not raining and an event occurs (someone falls) just as it begins to rain you now have a case of multiple events as mentioned earlier. The fall and the rain are both events occurring at the same time. Conditions are factors that need to be taken into consideration in your evaluation when you make your decision.

Some conditions:
• Environmental conditions (weather, terrain, wildlife)
• Time (time of day/night and seasons)
• Individuals present (Physical, Physiological & Emotional needs)

In general the entire environment in which you find yourself are your conditions. If any condition changes it will usually be considered an event at that time. Again, events that have been dealt with usually become part of your existing conditions.

CLS –Event
There is an obvious fork in the trail forcing a decision.
*(**Awareness** - I saw the fork)*

Evaluate

The second step in the DMP is gathering and prioritizing information. You will be using your lens to recognize and decide what is relevant before prioritizing that information. Part of your evaluation will be deciding how serious this event is by itself or how it compares to multiple events occurring at the same time.

Evaluate the Event

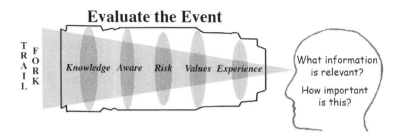

A culprit to contend with while effectively trying to evaluate an event is assumptions. We all make assumptions. Most of the time they are a result of past experiences. I think of assumptions as mini-decisions that have already been made that may or may not be correct. The problem is, if you proceed and they are not true, you may be building a decision on a shaky foundation. Faulty assumptions are a poor start to the DMP so beware. You know what is said when you assume, " It makes an ass out of you and me (ass-u-me)."

Believing someone is feeling a certain way instead of asking; using a log to cross the river without testing it; skiing over a snow bridge or walking onto a frozen lake without evaluating them first; taking for granted your stoves are working now because they worked two years ago are just some of the many assumptions that can lead to serious situations.

CLS – Evaluation
*Trail 1 is longer than Trail 2. Since I can read a topological (topo') map and I have the one for this area, it shows trail 1 has greater elevation gains and losses. (**Knowledge & Skills –** map reading) It is 10 AM. I need to be back at 6 PM (**Commitment** – Time restraints). I am feeling physically strong, confident and I am in good spirits (**Physical, Physiological, Psychological & Emotional Status** - all good). I am well equipped (day pack, food, water, first aid kit, headlamp, raincoat, some clothing layers, sunscreen, bug spray, bear spray, sunglasses, visor, hiking poles, hiking shoes, cell phone & whistle) with plenty of food and water.*

(**Experience** – What to bring on my hike). The weather is pleasant with a good forecast. (**Experience** – checking forecast.) My typical day hiking pace on level ground is 3 miles per hour. (**Experience** – calculated from numerous previous hikes) Risks involved appear to be low and acceptable because I believe my skills are more than adequate for the hike, given the conditions and the anticipated terrain. (**Risk Assessment & Experience**)

My lens for this step engaged the factors I have highlighted in **bold letters**. I feel I have given all of these factors equal priority because they seem equally relevant.

The input gathered could be different if I were to change some of my lens-factors. If my knowledge did not include the ability to read a topo' map I would not know that trail 1 has significant elevation gain and loss, which will alter my typical hiking pace. If I did not know the weather forecast, weather issues could arise. As mentioned earlier, if my awareness was compromised I may have missed the fork altogether. These are just a few examples how gathering information can change as your lens changes.

Goals

Before you make a decision you need to have an idea of what you would like to accomplish by your actions. Any and all of your lens-factors will be used to decide your goals. As mentioned before, not all of those factors will be in harmony. You may have opposing factors. You will have to prioritize your lens-factors and goals when choosing.

Know My Goals

Remember what I said about intense anger filters? If you can convert your anger from a filter to a non-priority lens-factor your process will be less emotional. To be honest with you, if I am pissed, I let that anger list some of my goals and options. I do this because it is one of my techniques for reducing my anger. I imagine horrible things I would like to see happen but I don't consider them as viable goals, options or actions. Since I am human I have feelings. The key is to try to rise above your strong emotions. I am sure there are times when emotional goals are appropriate, but in my experience I found strong emotional responses did not lead to my best decisions. Again, I have added some ways to reduce and possibly control emotions in *Appendix 2*.

When you state a goal you make a definitive choice of what you want to happen. That is different from saying you prefer something to happen. I listed preferences as a lens-factor because it affects the DMP. Just because you prefer one item to another, it does not become your choice until you select it.

I have certain preferences, which could become goals if I were to say, "I want to do this" instead of "I prefer to do this". I prefer to hike cross-country than staying on the main trail. I prefer panoramic views for my pictures. Even though I have not stated these as goals, these preferences may come into play when I choose options.

CLS – Goals
- *To get to Clear Lake and back before 6PM. (**Commitment** - another appointment)*
- *Spend at least one hour at the lake (**Desire & Experience** – want to enjoy a nice lunch at the lake and I know I need one hour before the hike out).*
- *Get a good workout (**Desire & Physical Status** – I want to maintain my hiking endurance).*
- *Doing a loop rather than seeing the same scenery by taking the same trail in and out (**Desire** – I really enjoy doing loops when I hike).*

- *I also have a **Preference**, if it is possible, of getting some panoramic pictures from a ridge one half mile above Trail 1.*

When I refocused my lens to make a list for my **Goals,** a few lens-factors changed and I did prioritize them. I put more weight on my time commitment. Doing a loop was next. My workout was third. My one-hour stay at the lake, while important, was my last concern. As I listed my goals, my preference for pictures whispered in my ear, but it was still not a listed goal.

Options

Listing your options is based upon you goals. Your lens will help you recognize and develop viable options - those you have the ability to execute and that do meet those goals.

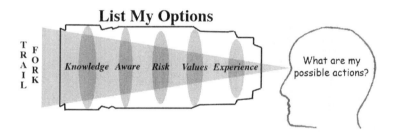

Here again, a filter will directly affect your options. Your boss tells you to do something that all of your being hates to do. You may have many options but your commitment to your job (job filter) only allows one option.

While I was listing and considering my options (A – D), which were based on my stated goals, I did not include my picture preference. However I saw each option had some extra time. While reading the topo' map (during evaluation) I noticed a ridgeline paralleled trail 1, but required an off trail route to get there (**Awareness**). The slope appeared to be reasonable on the map for leaving the trail and returning to it (**Skills** –map reading). After calculating the extra time available, I decided to change my picture **Preference** to a

46

Desire, which I added to my original goals. Now that I had the desire for pictures as a goal I added option E.

CLS – Options
A - Take Trail 1 in and out, which is 17.0 miles round trip with the most elevation gain and loss. Estimated hiking time will be almost 6 hours. With one hour at the lake I will be back at 5 PM, leaving 1 hour of extra time or less because my pace slows a bit going uphill. This option is cutting the time really close.

B - Take Trail 1 in and Trail 2 out at 13.5 miles round trip. Estimated hiking time 4.5 hours. With one hour at the lake I will be back at 3:30 PM, which leaves 2.5 hours of extra time. Taking the shorter and easier trail out for the last leg of the hike when I will be more fatigued. I have lots of extra time for a slower uphill pace.

C - Take Trail 2 in and Trail 1 out at 13.5 miles round trip. Estimated hiking time 4.5 hours. With one hour at the lake I will be back at 3:30 PM, which leaves 2.5 hours of extra time. Longer trail out for the last leg of the hike with greater elevation gain and loss when I am more fatigued. I have lots of extra time for the slower uphill pace.

D - Take Trail 2 in and out, which is 10.0 miles round trip. Estimated hiking time will be about 3.3 hours. With one hour at the lake I will be back about 2:20 PM, which leaves 3.6 hours of extra time.

E - Take Trail 1 in part of the way. Then go off trail up to the ridgeline for the panoramic pictures. Follow the ridgeline and drop back down to Trail 1. Take Trail 2 out. Estimated 1 additional mile for 14.5 miles round trip. Estimated hiking time 5 hours. With one hour at the lake I will be back at 4:00 PM, which leaves 2.0 hours of extra time with a shorter trail out for the last leg of the hike. These extra 2.0 hours allows a nice time cushion if I miscalculated my off trail excursion.

Action

This part of the DMP means you choose your option and act on it. Since choosing and acting are definitive, you need to have the ability to do so. I am sure you know people who take forever to make a choice and then still seem to wait to the last second to act on it. In addition, there are those who cannot act or even make a choice.

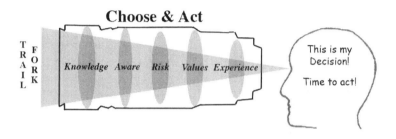

One of the important factors involved in taking action is your self-confidence, which I touched upon when defining ego. If you feel good about yourself and trust yourself, you'll be less likely to hesitate when choosing and taking action. Not acting when it is called for, out of the fear of being wrong, is a result of not trusting yourself and/or your self-image not accepting being wrong. Having strong self-confidence helps you make the tough call and to accept the consequences and the responsibilities if you are wrong.

Even though this ability to choose and act is important to everyone, it is even more important for those who lead others in outdoor settings. Decisions made in the outdoors have a greater potential of being serious and/or life threatening. If you cannot make these types of decisions you should not put yourself into the position of being responsible for the well-being of others.

Non-actions

I want to say a quick word about non-actions. There are two main types of non-actions.

1. *A result of one's inability to act.* Some reasons could be indecision, paralyzing fear, hesitation and/or, as

mentioned earlier, you missed the event. Regardless of the reason, you did not take action. Whether intentional or not, you will be dealing with the consequences of not acting;

2. *A proactive choice.* This non-action is actually a choice and an action. You have decided to do nothing with respect to the event. You have gone through the DMP and the option you chose was - not to act - at this time or at all. If you know you are going to act, but you are waiting for the appropriate moment, your postponed action is patience or as some prefer, timing. You still monitor your results to see if your decision is getting your expected results. If not, then repeat the process as mentioned before.

I raise this point because I have often seen novices feel the need to do something when nothing needs to be done, especially with trip leaders. Unseasoned leaders often feel they need to take action for any and all events. There are times when it is appropriate to do nothing. Understanding group dynamics can be very useful if you lead others. Part of that process includes the group establishing its norms. Sometimes those norms are set through friction in the group. Knowing when to step in is a skill a leader needs to develop. Sometimes you need to let the participants work through their differences without your interference.

Another reason for not doing something could be your values and/or beliefs. When my godson Alex turned eighteen I wanted to give him the gift of adventure. I told him I would pay for a roundtrip ticket to Europe and a Eurail Pass. He said he would prefer to go on an adventure with me. I decided to take him on the Hawaii kayaking trip I was leading. This was at a time in his life when Alex was not yet an outdoor enthusiast.

Part of our trip was paddling and camping along Hawai'i's rugged Na Pali Coast of Kaua'i. On the paddle out, Alex was zigzagging his way down the coast. I had already given him the necessary instruction on how to steer. I knew from experience that he just needed time to figure it out. Hadley, my fiancée, came over to me to tell me that Alex was really getting upset. I told her he was doing okay. The second time she came over she said, "If you don't do something, I will." I told her, "This is a learning and growth experience for Alex so trust me and please don't interfere." I explained to her that I was monitoring his frustration levels. I added, "He needs to do this on his own." She paddled off in a huff. That evening the group had dinner at Pizza Hut during which time Alex looked at me and said, "The paddle out was the hardest thing I have ever done. I feel so good I was able to do it on my own."

The goals in my process were to allow Alex the opportunity of growth through hard work and self-exploration. Hadley's goal was to minimize Alex's frustration. My goal required a non-action to his struggle. Hadley's action by going over to help Alex may have relieved his frustration but possibly taken away his sense of accomplishment. When I started my guiding career I stepped in too often or too early. In time, and through changes in my values, I got better at non-acting to certain events.

A more serious example is the number one mistake made by untrained responders, which is moving a victim or moving them too much. I once saw a bike accident on campus as I was heading to lunch. As I ran towards the gal on the ground, a young man lifted her up and carried her over to the lawn and laid her down before I could yell out, "Don't move her!" As in most injury situations, a full body check should have been done and only moved her if her immediate safety was an issue. There was no safety issue where she was located. Knowing when to act and not to act is a skill developed over time though experience.

Default actions

All of us have numerous default actions we have learned through training (skills) and others we have honed over years of decisions and experiences. Some people may call some of these default actions trained reflexes. The vast majority of the time our default actions serve us well. However, once in a while they don't. Most drivers go right to the brake when anything seems amiss. There are some times when using the accelerator will be the best way to avoid a problem on the road. However, most drivers have braking as their default action, even before they assess the situation.

I am not saying having these automatic responses is bad. In fact they are usually more efficient. Just be aware they exist and more importantly, know yours.

CLS – Action
Due to my original stated goals for my Clear Lake hike, I chose option B for the following reasons:
- *I wanted to do a loop. (**Desire**);*
- *I want to hike more than option D, which is only 10.0 miles (**Desire**);*
- *The 13.5 miles of option B will be a good workout (**Physical Status**);*
- *Harder hike to the lake, but easier return when energy stores get lower (**Experience** – knowing my body's performance from past hikes).*

I assigned greater weight to my loop desire when making this choice.

*However, when I decided to amend my goals to go off trail with the hope of getting those pictures (**Preference**) I was able to create option E, which became my added choice for the day. I felt my map reading skills, sense of direction and hiking ability would fit the anticipated terrain of option E (**Skills & Risk Management**). I also calculated that I would have enough extra time in case my estimates were off. (Time to do it and still honor my previous **Commitment**).*

I chose option E because I realized my desire for pictures became my top priority. In addition, my other goals were still being met.

Snap judgments
Most likely you have heard the phrase "snap judgment." I am guessing it had a negative connotation attached to it, such as,

"Don't make any snap judgments." The word "snap" implies very quick. Is anything wrong with making quick decisions? Not if they need to be made in a hurry, such as a life-threatening situation.

When being criticized for making snap judgments, it is not the speed of the decision that is being questioned; it is the quality of the decision. If decisions are being made without considering important factors, then the criticism may be warranted. If you have time and are a person who frequently makes those snap decisions, perhaps you should allow yourself a moment to ask, "Have I really considered the most important factors?" In my experience, the most common criticism of "snappers" is, "They were not thinking about the impact on others."

Fail-safe
Before we leave this step I want you to consider the **Action** part of the process as your fail-safe window. If time permits, here are a few fail-safe questions:
- Am I rushing my decision?
- Should I get another perspective?
- How will I look back on this decision?
- Is there a filter over my lens?
- Am I repeating an ineffective DMP habit? (This will be discussed soon)

If you feel you are rushing your decision, take a breath and ask, "What's the hurry?" Try to determine why you feel rushed.

Up until now, I have been presenting the DMP with you being the only one involved in making the decision. I did this to present the concepts in a less complicated manner. For now, I am adding getting another perspective (input from others) as one of your *fail-safe* options, even though you can ask for that input during any or all of the steps in the DMP. I will discuss group decision making later, in the "Leaders-Participants-Groups" chapter.

This is when you need to use your future hindsight lens-factor. You are trying to imagine how you are going to view your decision in the future. *"Why might I regret this decision?"* is a good question to ask.

With respect to filters, if strong emotions (anger, fear, hate), commitments (boss, family, religion), ego (peer pressure, self image) or any other factors are erratically driving your decision, you have to re-evaluate.

There have been a number of times in my life when I was very emotional and decided to write a letter to the individual at the root of those emotions. Through experience I learned that sending emotional letters never got the results I really wanted other than to vent my feelings. Now, before sending an emotional letter, I wait a day and read it to see if I still want to send it - then I wait a few more days! Finally, after a few weeks I found that after reading the letter again, I no longer had a need to send it. This was my fail-safe period.

In the case of sending a letter, you may have lots of time. Since many decisions involving safety need to be made sooner than later, especially in the outdoors, you may not have that same luxury. However, and if possible, you still need to do one last fail-safe check before you act.

If your fail-safe checks appear to be a non-issue, then act. I must add, learning how to recognize, and more importantly, rise above strong emotions is a skill that will bring about or help make better decisions.

Results
Once your action is taken you need to monitor to see if you are getting your anticipated results. Your final outcome should be an **effective decision**, which is when your **attained goals truly address the needs of the event**. It is important to note that there are times when your actions will not properly deal with the event. In which case you will have to try again.

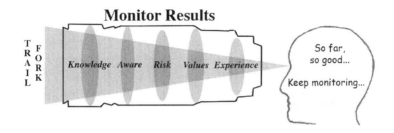

Monitor Results

TRAIL
FORK

Knowledge   Aware   Risk   Values   Experience

So far, so good...

Keep monitoring...

Remember, a decision you make right now is based upon the information you have at that moment and your lens-factors. Once the decision to act is made, those factors and/or environment can change in an instant, which may require another decision.

CLS – Results
*As I hiked to Clear Lake via option E, I regularly checked to see if my actions were taking me towards my stated goals. Everything was fine until I came to a series of cliff faces near the top of the ridgeline that did not show on the topo' map, which is now an added event while I am monitoring my decision to get to the ridgeline. I quickly decided I did not want to assume the risk (**Risk Perception**) of the climb and decided to drop back down to Trail 1 and continue as if I chose option B. As a result, I never achieved my goal of getting the pictures, but I did achieve the other goals mentioned.*

In this case the new event was the cliff face. My evaluation was that I needed climbing gear to continue up the cliff, which I didn't have (**Risk Assessment**). Climbing was not one of my goals, especially alone. In this case my **risk assessment** took a higher priority over my **desire** of getting pictures. I needed to change my actions because I reprioritized my goals.

Now that my circumstances and location have changed I need to redo my decision. This time the DMP is quicker. I realize options C and D are no longer viable since I went a good distance along Trial #1. Option A was cutting the time too close so the added time spent going off trail makes it a non-option. Since my other goals did not change, option B is my choice. There are other potential options such as returning to the trailhead if time was an issue or if I felt too tired to get to the lake. If I was feeling that an overwhelming disappointment filter was covering my lens, and thus affecting my other goals, I may just say forget it and head out and go to the nearest pub. Again, option B won.

Once you make a decision regarding an event, time moves on. During that time new events can occur, which will require new decisions or altering decisions you have already made. These are among the reasons why you are regularly checking your results.

The factors I used in my lens for options E & B were my desires, past experience, time commitment, self-awareness, my skills, environmental conditions, my risk assessment, physical status, physiological status and psychological status.

I have just demonstrated the **Reactive DMP** seen through my lens. How did it compare to your response? Since there is really no right or wrong answer, the question you need to ask yourself is, "Did my results achieve my goals and did my goals deal with the event to my satisfaction?" If your answer is "yes," you have performed an effective decision.

If you think this is all nonsense perhaps you should follow the decision-making advice of Yogi Berra when he said, "When you come to a fork in the road, take it!"

Use It or Lose It
Now that I have reviewed the DMP using my lens, you can see how involved the process can be. As you make more decisions you learn how to do this process more quickly and hopefully more effectively. I have learned that making decisions can be a skill in itself. Like all skills, the more you practice them the smoother they become. "Use it or lose it" also applies to making decisions.

If you have not been involved in an outdoor activity for a few years, your DMP for that activity may be rusty. On the flip side, your increased maturity and experiences may be an asset. I personally believe my decision-making process has improved with age. However, I also know that I have forgotten and/or lost certain abilities over those same years. It is clear to me I would not jump into a class IV-V river until I refreshed my whitewater kayaking skills. The wisdom of aging, has taught me, that my brain still wants to write checks my body can no longer cash.

Here is an example of me losing it because I didn't use it. It is also a good example of not being truly in touch with my lens-factors. In December of 2014, at age 64, I met my outdoor buddies (Tom, Lee and Paul) in Squaw Valley, California. We planned an overnight X-C ski trip to a Sierra Club hut in the Sierra Nevada mountain range. I figured I had not been on X-C skis in about twenty-five years. Given we were following a Forest Service road all the way to the cabin I assumed even my rusty skills could handle it. The uphill part was easy with my climbing skins on my skis. The snow was icy, hard packed and well traveled. We stopped for lunch at the top of a rise.

After lunch our route took a short drop around some turns before climbing to the cabin. I took my skins off to go downhill because the slope wasn't steep enough to ski with the skins still on. To my surprise that short drop was close to being one of the more terrifying experiences in my life (and I have done some scary @#$%!). Two years earlier I had a total knee and hip replacement. Even though my legs felt strong I did not feel any control over my skis - and not because of those replaced joints. My skills felt like they had disappeared, but my brain was still telling me "You could do this!" Unfortunately my brain was remembering my four, week-long, Trans-Sierra ski trips decades earlier, with one being the high route, where I was skiing up and down extremely steep slopes with a pack weighing at least 60 lbs. My brain thought nothing of this bunny slope of a road. Yet my body no longer had the skills necessary for me to feel any control. My lens was not serving me well that day.

*After spending a great night with my friends at the hut I knew
I would not be comfortable skiing out. I had visions of my ski
tips crossing, me going over and dislocating my hip. Since the
snow was mostly firm and not too deep I decided to just walk
out carrying my skis. My buddies skied out.*

As I hiked, I felt very good about my decision. My ego seemed
to be fine. Aside from enjoying the scenery, most of my
thoughts were focused on the aging process. I was beginning
to accept the fact that I was no longer the backcountry skier I
once was two decades earlier. Maybe it would have been
different if I continued to ski over those years? My friends
had been skiing all these years and they were OK. Even Tom,
who is several years older than me was fine. Instead, I had
chosen to spend those years sea kayaking.

The experience confirmed my beliefs about "Use it or lose it".
What was most important to me was that I had not let my
ego or concern for reputation dictate my actions. I
recognized I was a mere mortal, an awareness I rarely had
when I was younger. Factors in my lens were adjusting. In
the end, I was proud of my decision to walk out. My primary
goal was to spend quality time with my friends, which I did.
In retrospect my best course of action should have been to
go in and out on snowshoes since I had no idea of my skiing
ability after a twenty-year hiatus.

During the long drive home, from Squaw Valley to Seattle, I
reflected on the entire weekend. My initial feeling was that of
loss with respect to my skiing abilities.

I was not only growing older, I was older. My frame of mind
completely turned around as I listened to John Denver
singing *Poems, Prayers and Promises* where he says; "It turns
me on to think of growing old." A smile broadened across my
face as I reflected on the rich life I had enjoyed - full of
fantastic adventures. Instead of measuring what I can no
longer do, I focused on how much more I still want to do.

Mistakes/Misjudgments

You are going to make errors in judgment, which means you did not get the results you anticipated. Whether you call them mistakes, misjudgments, errors or any other term that means, "You were wrong," some of them will be minor and some may include injury or death. You need to prepare yourself for how you will deal with your serious mistakes. In fact, sometimes things just happen, but as a leader you may still feel it was your fault.

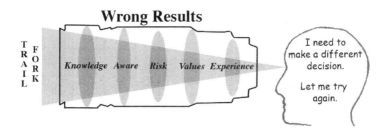

By playing basketball in High School and College I learned how to deal with mistakes. During a game, you do not have the luxury of sulking when you missed a shot or if you fouled another player. The game is still going and even a split second hesitation can make a difference. I had to learn the hard way, not to stop and look at the referee if I know I fouled an opponent. If I just kept playing sometimes I avoided the penalty.

There will be plenty of time for regret, self-retribution and self-pity later. You can wallow all you want in the privacy of your tent or at home. If you are in a difficult situation you need to focus on that situation and not get distracted by being wrong. If you are leading a trip, your personal feelings should not interfere with your responsibilities, especially in an emergency. If someone gets injured, you need to be on the top of your game to deal with it, not clouding your DMP or your responsibilities with a filter of guilt. Learning from your mistakes happens during reflection.

In addition, since we live in a very litigious society, you need to keep your mouth shut with respect to taking or assigning blame. All too often, leaders mistakenly feel they are responsible for everything that happens on their trip. Really? You think you are responsible for someone tripping on the trail, being bitten by a snake, falling into a river and drowning or getting seriously burned by falling into a campfire? Even if you are at fault, if and when the authorities question you, tell the truth as to what you saw. Do not say, "It was my fault, because I should have seen it coming or prevented it." As I said earlier, "Don't "*should*" all over yourself." Some professional guides have told me, that their insurance companies have told them not to say anything until they speak to legal council.

To err is human; forgiveness and blame come later.

Pointing Fingers - As I said, "You are going to make mistakes." Accept responsibility and own up to it. It is part of making decisions. These mistakes are learning experiences. Unfortunately, in this lawsuit happy world, pointing fingers has taken the place of accepting responsibility. My Aikido Sensei once told me, "When you point your finger at someone else, there are three more fingers pointing back at you."

Common Reasons For Misjudgments
Aside from learning the lessons from each mistake, you can learn even more if you look at your mistakes collectively. Try to identify any re-occurring reasons for your mistakes, such as always making snap judgments. Even though there are numerous reasons for making errors, here are some of the more common ones I have seen over the years:
- Filter over your lens (usually strong emotion or values);
- Didn't get all the facts (missed items to consider);
- Ignorance (just didn't know);
- Assumptions vs. facts;
- Snap judgments (didn't take enough time before acting);
- Indecision (waited too long to act);
- Inadequate training;

- Overwhelmed (Anxiety &/or panic);
- Ego/reputation concerns (worrying how you will be judged).

If you do identify re-occurring reasons ("ineffective DMP habits") for your past poor judgments, then you can take steps to change your behavior. At the very least, I suggest you add your ineffective DMP habits to your fail-safe list of questions.

Compromise

Compromise is defined as an agreement or a settlement of a dispute that is reached by each side making concessions. When discussing values in the *Decision-Making Lens* chapter, I mentioned the possibility of conflicting values. It is not uncommon to have conflict within or between your lens-factors. If you do, then it is up to you to prioritize the importance of your factors. This act of choosing - one over the other - is a form of self-compromise. When you see your results or look back on that decision, you will find out if your compromise was worth it. It is not easy when you have to choose between strongly held values or beliefs. I have found it is easier to compromise desires and preferences.

If your decision involves one or more individuals and they have a rightful say in the DMP, then there will be times when there will be conflict between your chosen action and the chosen action(s) of those involved. Their chosen actions are just as valid as yours, unless you have previously determined which one of you has the final say when there are conflicting decisions.

I raise the issue of compromise because it is a double-edged sword. It is great if those involved can decide on a win-win solution even though your original decisions conflicted. There is a reason why people say, "Two heads are better than one." A decision made by two or more brings more to the table, which can lead to a richer decision.

Unfortunately, that is not usually the case. More times than not, concessions need to be made in the name of compromise. The question I want you to consider is, "When does too much compromise become too much?" How often can you compromise your values and beliefs before it negatively affects you? That line does exist. Unfortunately, many folks don't see that line until they have crossed it. If you have a clear understanding of your values and beliefs, then you may have a better idea of how far you are willing to go in the name of compromise.

Regardless of how and when you compromise with others, once you agree to it the responsibility of that decision is partially yours - on paper. I can tell you from experience, you will be taking 100% of it in your mind the moment you think, "I should not have compromised."

I am not even suggesting that you avoid compromise because you do not live in a vacuum. Compromising is a fact of life. I am just asking you to pay attention and try to be true to yourself whenever possible.

Reflection
Part of the *Experiential Learning* concept is reflection. Much of our true learning comes when we take the time to look back on our actions and ask, "What have I learned from this experience?" There are many lessons to be learned, if you take the time to reflect.

Unfortunately, in this over connected electronic society, we do not allow ourselves any time to be alone in our thoughts in order to reflect. Perhaps I should create a reflection app, which forces individuals to take some time to process the day's events. I encourage you to make time for yourself, to learn the lessons you may be missing. Since *history has a habit of repeating itself,* do you want to make the same mistakes because you did not learn from the first one?

After you make your decision, regardless of the outcome, you will have to live with the consequences of the actions you take. I believe you will be your biggest critic, if you are a person who takes responsibility for what you do. As mentioned earlier, you will have people judging your actions. How you respond to those comments will be a result of how strongly you feel about your actions. You can never please everyone. The question that really matters is, "Did you satisfy yourself, as a result of your actions?"

As a reminder, the reactive DMP is for events that are occurring or have occurred. You were presented with a situation and you needed to react. Your ability to anticipate events will improve with experience, which means, you may be able to avoid situations instead of having to react to them.

Let me share a way that helps me remember the DMP steps (EEGOAR). I could not find better names for each step that would give me an easy-to-remember acronym such as HOMES, which is an acronym for the names of the five Great Lakes (**H**uron, **O**ntario, **M**ichigan, **E**rie & **S**uperior). Therefore I use "brain-paddle" to remember the first letter of each step. A **brain** test is an EEG and a **paddle** is OAR. I also tried EEGOAR pronounced with a long E at the beginning and I think of Dr. Frankenstein's helper. These two help me; I hope they work for you. If not, try to find a way that does.

CHAPTER 4

DECISION-MAKING PROCESS
PROACTIVE DECISIONS

As the Director of Adventure Programs at UCSB I learned that anticipating events was the best skill I could develop. Since the outdoor environment is so dynamic, one will always need to react to unexpected events. However, the more time you put into anticipating and planning, I can assure you, the less often you will find yourself in serious situations. Many of the decisions you will have to face on a typical outing can be made before the event. If you anticipate effectively, you will even have responses in place to deal with emergency events. The key is being proactive.

There are two different types of proactive decisions. The first requires **immediate** action and the second **postpones** action. If you believe that current conditions (environment or actions of others) may lead to an event you would prefer to avoid, then it requires immediate action. If you are looking towards the future then you will be postponing your actions until later. It is important to note that decisions with postponed actions need to be flexible because when and if it comes time to act, the existing conditions may require a different decision.

Patience is a perfect example of the proactive DMP with postpones actions. You know what you will probably do or say, but you are going to wait until the right time. Some people have incredible patience while others cannot wait to take action. I feel there is a time for either, depending on the situation.

The major difference between the reactive and the proactive decision-making process is in the event phase. Recognizing the event is the challenge because you are looking for things that could happen, but may not happen. Once you have identified the event the rest of the DMP is the same whether reactive or proactive.

When I was in college taking my methods of teaching class, my instructor, Jack Kaminer, (also my basketball coach) instilled in me a very valuable lesson. In an assignment, we had to respond to how we would handle a specific situation while teaching in a New York City high school in a tough neighborhood. The scenario said, "While on hall duty you hear a noise in the men's room and you go in." When I read the scenario, my inner-city survival instincts said I shouldn't walk into the men's room by myself. I said I wouldn't get into this situation in the first place; however since you put me in the men's room by myself, this is what I would do.

There were about thirty of us in the class. When Jack handed back the assignments he said, "out of thirty of you only two in the class responded as I hoped, which was not to go into the men's room by yourself. He hammered into to us to "not to get into the situation in the first place." This was an instance where my gut feeling was an asset.

I have learned the greatest asset an outdoor adventurer can develop is to recognize and stay clear of the situations in the first place. If it is predictable, it may be avoidable. If you cannot avoid it, then at the very least, you can try to prepare for it. Learning to anticipate means looking ahead.

Potential Events (Anticipation)
In the reactive DMP all you have to do is recognize the event. In comparison, being proactive means you have to anticipate, which is the ability to foresee potential events. You actually enter the world of make-believe when you do this. You are playing the "What if?" game.

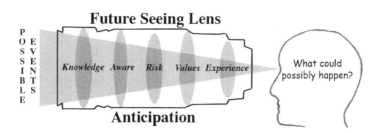

64

In the planning phase, many times in the comfort of your home, you are trying to anticipate possible events so you can have postponed actions in place for a successful adventure with an eye on avoiding serious and/or harmful events.

Once you are on your adventure you will be watching out for and trying to avoid the potential events you identified and the ones you haven't. Actually being there will give you more input because there will be factors you did not take into consideration during your planning with respect to postponed actions. You will be evaluating the new input and adjusting your decisions accordingly.

As an example, if I saw a trip participant carving a marshmallow roasting stick, cutting towards their body instead of away, I would identify this as a potential injury event which I feel needs immediate action - informing the person of the possible dangers of their technique. Even though they may have never gotten injured, I saw the potential based upon past experience.

With respect to identifying events, your lens works in many ways. There are times where you may get subtle messages that an event is pending. You don't know what it is, but you get a feeling.

Pre-event alert
It would be great to have psychic abilities. Sometimes you may feel like you do because all of your senses are sending you messages and the input leads you to sense an impending event. You don't know exactly what it is but you just feel like something is going to happen.

I do not discount the possibility of pre-cognition. However, I need to focus on the abilities of the average person. These so-called *pre-event feelings* can be any number of things. Your senses hear it, see it, feel it but you do not understand the message. However your conscious mind is now on a heightened alert. It could be sounds beyond your normal hearing range yet the brain detects it. It could be changes in air pressure felt by your ears but not noticeable to your conscious thought process. Your senses are working 24/7. As humans we only use a small portion of our brain's capacity so we may not be able to quantify or identify these signals, but our brain puts us on notice.

I have learned to tune into my environment. When I do, I begin see and feel a flow/pattern to my surroundings. When that rhythm is disrupted, I notice it. Oftentimes that disruption is a subtle hint before the event. When it is in a movie, you get that *eerie* music. In the outdoors, it could be the sudden quiet when the birds stop singing. Whatever it is, I suggest you learn how to tune into your surroundings and notice the patterns.

On a scouting trip for a future Lake Powell kayak tour, my buddy Don & I spent the night in a car camping area next to the lake in December. The Halls Crossing campground was flat (dirt & gravel) with zero trees in the high deserts of Utah. We both slept outside without tents because even though it was very cold, it was bone dry. I was cozy in my -40 degree down bag on my sleeping pad placed upon a tarp. At early morning light I felt a need to wake up because my brain was sensing something. I opened my eyes and at my feet was a curious coyote standing on my tarp. He was motionless but looking right at me.

After we shared looks for a minute or two, I wished him "good morning," thinking the sound of my voice would spook him and he would take off. Instead he just stood there on all four legs looking at me. Since I am 6'7" tall I was hoping he was thinking that this giant wrap in front of him was too big of a breakfast burrito for him to handle and he would wander off to find a smaller meal. Come to think of it, Don was much shorter. Since he didn't appear to be threatening and I was still tired, I decided to close my eyes and go back to sleep. It was also too cold (6 degrees) to get out of my bag at that time. Why did I wake up? I have been awakened by noises before. This was different. My body was sensing something and sent me an alert.

Some people describe this intuition as their "gut feeling." For the purposes of this book I am going to differentiate between the pre-event alert and one's gut feeling. The pre-event alert is that feeling that something is going to happen. I used "gut feeling" for that intangible feeling we have during and after we make the decision, which I discussed in the *Decision-Making Lens* chapter.

As mentioned above, identifying and/or anticipating events are the key to proactive decisions. How and why you foresee them can be for many reasons, all of which are a result of your lens. Here are a few examples:
- An unchecked situation presently occurring;
- Memories of past experiences;
- Wealth of knowledge;
- Warnings in guidebooks or from locals;
- Reliable forecasts;
- Previous behavior/traits of others involved.

Regardless of how you identify a potential event, once identified, you follow the remaining steps of the DMP to decide how to avoid the event or possible ways to deal with it if it occurs.

Proactive Decision With Immediate Action
Scenario: You are on a picnic with your family near a fast moving river with lots of rapids.

Potential event *– Your child could fall into the river because he or she is playing too close to the edge.*

Evaluate *– You determine this as a high-risk situation, which requires an **immediate action** to prevent the event.*

Goal *– To keep your child from falling in the river.*

Options *– Move them away from the river. Stay with them while they play.*

Actions – *You decide to rush over and pull them back from the river's edge so they don't fall in. This is an immediate action for a proactive decision to prevent the potential event of falling into the river.*

Results – *Your child is now playing far enough from the river's edge according to your comfort zone (risk-management factor)*

In reality, your child could have played there all day and never fallen in. However, your lens-factors determined you did not want to take that chance so you decided to act.

Proactive Decision With Postponed Action

Let's look at making *proactive decisions with postponed actions* using the river scenario that has your child playing by the river's edge.

Having heard of numerous accounts of people slipping into fast moving rivers, you are very aware this is a potential event on your upcoming trip. Since one of your ongoing goals in life is your child's safety, you identify falling in the river as a **potential event** *you wish to avoid.*

You **evaluate** *this as a high priority event because you child's life could be in danger and you know your child is curious and loves water.*

Your **goals** *are very clear: keep your child from slipping into the river; educating them in how to avoid falling in.*

Here are a few of the many **options** *to achieve your goals.*
1. *You can explain to your child the dangers of falling in.*
2. *You can take them by the hand and show them the possible dangers and then bring them back to an acceptable location.*
3. *You can set a boundary line they shouldn't cross.*
4. *You can tie a rope to them to keep them a certain distance from the river.*
5. *You can require them to wear a PFD when near the river.*

68

There are many other options, each with the goal of educating them and keeping them from drowning in the river.

*Since you cannot take the action now, because you are just planning, whatever option you choose will be a **postponed action**. However, after identifying your options you realize that you may need to add certain items onto your equipment list as suggested in options 4 & 5.*

Should you finally take your postponed action, at that point you will have the opportunity to monitor you **results**.

Earlier I gave the example of a participant carving a marshmallow roasting stick in a manner that could have caused an injury. It was an example of a proactive decision, which I determined needed immediate action because he was in the midst of carving. If I used my anticipation skills to look farther ahead, I could have planned a mini-class for the group showing them the correct way to carve sticks prior to the campfire. Same potential event, but this time it would have been a postponed action. By doing so, the incorrect carving event would probably never happen. I say probably because, demonstrating a skill and expecting everyone to follow the example are two different things. That is why you still have to monitor the action.

I must reiterate the need to be flexible with postponed actions because you were not facing the event in real time under real conditions when you made your proactive decision.

One of the many aspects I like about future decisions is the time delay which allows me to revisit my postponed actions to see if the factors I chose for my lens have changed or how I prioritized them. If they have, I will change my future actions accordingly. The extra time also gives me a chance to explore, in more depth, many of my lens-factors, which helps me get more clarity of those factors.

Evaluating Potential Events
Once you have identified possible future events you will have the luxury of gathering and prioritizing that information with time on your side. Most of our reactive decisions have to be made quickly. Proactive ones (not requiring immediate action) allow us to use more lens-factors and give us time to gather more input.

Since you will be identifying many possible events you will need to prioritize those events.

Goals For Potential Events
I enjoy not being rushed when making plans because it gives me more time to think about, clarify and identify my goals. This extra time may give you the ability to see if one or more overpowering lens-factors or even a filter is dictating your goals.

Options For Potential Events
The luxury of time is often a blessing *and* a curse when it comes to identifying your options when dealing with future events. You will identify more options because you are not rushed, but then you have a longer list from which to choose.

There is another aspect of choosing options for your trip. Since you are focused and will be thinking of potential events, what happens if you get to your starting point and you cannot do the trip as planned? What now?

I learned a valuable lesson during a government shut down that occurred while running Adventure Programs. Upon returning from the trip, my two leaders informed me they had been denied access to the Colorado River due to the shut down. I was very proud of my staff because they immediately pulled out the maps of the area, which was required equipment, and found an alternative destination for the canoe trip.

I knew there was a shut down, but during my many years of running trips to this section of river, below Lake Mead, I have never seen a ranger on land or on the water. I knew it was part of a National Recreation Area but there are no entrance gates or fees collected. However, a ranger was at the put-in notifying users that the river was closed because they couldn't respond with emergency aid if needed. I found it ironic that the only time we ever saw a ranger; they were there to close the river. That experience taught me to identify alternative trips if unexpected changes occurred that prohibited the original trip destination, aside from a last minute check, to see if there are any closures. Since conditions can change, trailheads can close, roads can wash out, etc... I suggest you do the same rather than automatically canceling the trip and driving home. By doing so you will have planned for the alternative and not have to spend time determining if there is a second or third choice.

Actions For Potential Events
If you are planning ahead you will not be taking action, but rather setting the stage for taking action when and if it becomes necessary. Remember, these future decisions were made without having all of the input at the moment you will be acting. These future actions need to be reviewed once you are in the environment, so remain flexible. If your action still fits the event, goals and option chosen, you are then good to go. If not, adjust accordingly.

When you plan your itinerary, you create a proactive decision list of places you want to see, things you want to do and your timeline to make it happen. By putting that plan on paper, you have acted. Each item on that list is a postponed action. Since the trip has yet to happen, the premises on which you used to create this wish list may not exist at the time of or during the trip so, as mentioned numerous times before, your itinerary needs to be flexible.

Results
You cannot monitor results until you take action. When and if you do act, this step is the same, which is to determine whether or not you are getting your anticipated results.

One thing I do with my results is record them in my journal. I make note of the future events that actually happened from my list. I also list the events that happened that I did not anticipate for future reference. I learned writing them down helped me remember and reinforce the planning I have done. I am listing the results of my planning.

Trip Planning
When we plan a trip we are planning for future events, needs and desires. We research our routes, plan our meals, create equipment lists and itineraries and deal with many other details with the goal of getting the most out of our adventure. In the Clear Lake scenario, you found out about the hike after speaking with the ranger. The fork in the trail was our event that was unknown to us and necessitated a reactive decision.

What if you researched day hikes in your planning phase? The fork in the trail would have become known. In fact, you could have learned a lot more about the details of the hike and come to a decision as to which route you will take when you get to the park. Of course you will re-examine your decision the day of the hike once you know the weather conditions, trail restrictions if any, your time restraints and your physical status. As mentioned above, by recognizing future events you can make preliminary decisions before the event happens.

With the current availability of satellite imagery, on the Internet, you could have zoomed in on the ridgeline above Clear Lake and seen the rock faces. This would have completely eliminated your option E, or changed it to include bringing climbing gear to get up the rock face. That is, if you wanted to climb alone.

I cannot say enough about the planning opportunities now available due to the Internet and Google maps. I was able to find a huge clearing on Forest Service land for viewing the 2017 total solar eclipse right on the center line of totality. The location was far from crowds and I avoided the massive traffic jams experienced by many others.

I love planning trips to get the most out of my time. I also know all plans need to be flexible. There is nothing wrong with being spontaneous as in the Clear Lake scenario as I posed it. You got to the park. You felt like taking a hike. You briefly asked what day hikes were available. You chose Clear Lake because it was the closest trailhead. There was no planning and once you started hiking you found out you had to decide upon one of two main trails to get to the lake.

I have done hikes like this many times. I raise the point of future events to show there are other ways to decide your hike. If your desire is to take the best day hikes available in the park, then that lens-factor will be a priority and motivate you to explore your options and plan future events. If your desire is to be spontaneous then you may make very few plans. The more compelling factors in your lens will determine your actions.

Before we leave the DMP I want to share a few more of my values and experiences with you regarding decisions. I have often said, "There is only one decision in my life I wish I could change." That does not mean I haven't made poor decisions. I have made decisions that were bad in my eyes, ones I am ashamed of and others that were painful, but all of them combined have made me who I am today, so I would not change them. My greatest growth and lessons learned have been from all of my combined decisions. While I enjoy my successful decisions, I have appreciation for the ones that help me grow. If you are curious about that one decision I wish I could change, I have included it in *Appendix 3*.

I share this because you will have an opportunity to learn from every decision you make if you pay attention, acknowledge and accept that you will make errors. You should not avoid making decisions because you are afraid of making mistakes. You will make mistakes. However, if you learn from your mistakes, the percentage of success will increase as you make more decisions. If you do not get the outcome you anticipate, you will need courage to deal with and accept the consequences and responsibilities that come with your actions. If you are successful you can pat yourself on the back for a job well done.

It haunts me when I have missed an event that I should have seen coming, even if I deal with it successfully. Not being able to deal with the event effectively would be worse. I attribute my success rate to my lens-factors and possibly a little luck of the draw.

It is time to put your DMP to work to see what you do when faced with different challenges.

CHAPTER 5

COURSE OF ACTION SCENARIOS

It is time for you to practice your decision-making by playing, "What if?" These scenarios will help you think about and hopefully clarify your own lens-factors and focusing your **Lens** as you practice making decisions. If you commit your responses to writing, I believe you will get the most out of this exercise.

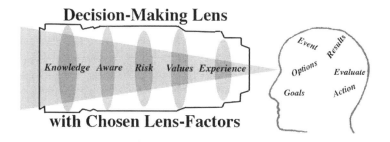

The next chapter reviews these scenarios. No fair peeking until you have written down your answers. Just for the record, almost all of the scenarios are based on real incidents with some minor changes.

For each scenario, write down the following:
- Identify the *EVENT(S);*
- *EVALUATE* by listing relevant input and prioritize;
- List your *GOALS;*
- List possible *OPTIONS;*
- *ACT* by committing to an option.

Scenario #1 - Head Wound
On a novice backpacking trip a person stumbles off the trail and falls down a rock slope. The hiker has a head wound with the usual heavy bleeding from the scalp. Upon examination you cannot see any obvious broken bones. At first, the patient is dizzy, scared and has blurred vision. After 20 minutes, the patient is well enough to be helped back to

camp. In camp the patient is still dizzy, has headaches and has disrupted vision. Your camp is two miles from the van. The nearest hospital is three hours away. It is 3pm, eight people are in the group and you are the only trip leader. What is your course of action?

Scenario #2 - Huge Surf
You and your friends have planned today's kayaking trip for a month. The weather is beautiful but the surf is huge. You perceive some of the group members are scared but not saying anything. One of the participants is elated because he loves surf. He is very verbal about it to the point where his enthusiasm is almost catching. You know some of the group members have never dealt with surf before. What is your course of action?

Scenario #3 - Group Dissent
You are the only leader of eight novice backpackers. The month is November and you are in a mountain top valley in southern California at elevation 6,000 ft. You have just reached this valley after a steep five-mile uphill hike from the van. Heavy storm clouds are moving in fast. It is 3pm and a conflict develops in the group. It is cold and the rain is starting. Four members of the group want to hike back down to the van and drive or hitchhike to the nearest motel. What is your course of action?

Scenario #4 - Bike Accident
You are one of the three leaders on a bike trip. You are on the trailing bike. You come to the bottom of a steep hill on a country road and after the turn you see one of the participants wiped out in the middle of the road. You see another participant about a quarter mile away riding back towards the accident. There is no one else to be seen at the moment. The victim is lying face down on the road, has serious road rash, and is moaning, crying, and not responding well to questions. What is your course of action?

Scenario #5 - Cave Kayaking

You and two others are leading a kayak tour around one of the Channel Islands off of the California coast. As the head guide for the day you are checking out the interior of a sea cave before you let the group enter. While in the cave alone, a big set of swells roll in and you find yourself being bashed into the back wall of the cave. As a result of the impact you get injured; are knocked out of your kayak and it is too painful for you to call for help. What is your course of action?

Scenario #6 - Trip Location Change

You decide to finally do that solo back county trip. You told your significant other your plans and when you would be home. When you get to the trailhead you find the route you want to take appears too risky due to posted bear attack signs. You decide to drive to another location a few hours away. There is no cell phone service at either location. While on your trip you get injured and cannot make your way back to the car. What is your course of action?

Scenario #7 - Equipment Failure

While leading a backpacking trip into the mountains you and your fellow leader discover that the two stoves you brought along are not working. You brought food that has to be cooked. Fires are strictly prohibited with a $5,000 fine. The ranger told you they are enforcing the "No Fire" restriction with full penalty because last month they lost 50,000 acres of original growth trees and the fire danger is still high. There are 12 very hungry backpackers who have hiked ten miles up to 10,000 ft. and the sun is setting. What is your course of action?

Scenario #8 - Behind Schedule

You are leading a beginner's canoe trip and the group is extremely slow. Most of the canoes are not maintaining a straight course. It takes you 5 hours to get to a lunch spot that normally takes 2 hours. Wind and current are adding to the difficulty of the canoeists. An hour after a very late lunch break you realize you will not reach your intended camp, with the hot springs, until well after dark. The air temperature is getting colder. It is November, you are in the Arizona/Nevada desert area and you are in a river canyon. What is your course of action?

Scenario #9 - Snow Slope
You and your two friends have been trying to get out for a one-day cross-country ski trip for the last month. The weekdays have been sunny, but each weekend there were heavy snowstorms so you kept postponing the trip. Finally the weather pattern changed and you have a favorable forecast. The weather turned out to be great. The three of you have been having a great day skiing in the backcountry. As all of you ski across an open slope, discussing the Seahawks game, you hear a strange sound as you feel the snow underneath your skis settle. What is your course of action?

Scenario #10 - Emergency Stop
You are driving your family to a long anticipated vacation on the water. You're cruising at the speed limit (60 mph) and you are towing boats on a trailer. Up ahead you see a minivan parked on the side of this two-lane road, which has a very wide shoulder. The passengers are out of the van and someone is changing a flat tire. There is traffic coming in the opposite direction. Just as you get close to the van a dog darts out right in front of your vehicle. What is your course of action?

Scenario #11 - No Sleeping Bag
You and two friends are packing your backpacks at the trailhead for a three-day outing. You suddenly realize you left your sleeping bag sitting in your garage. You are 5 hours from home and there is only one car. What is your course of action?

Scenario #12 - Different Agendas
You and your significant other are on your one-week summer vacation. You have been telling your partner about this location for the past few years and you are finally here. You wake up early and are rearing to get up and explore the

area, but your partner seems to be lounging in the tent. To your surprise, after a late breakfast, your partner sets up a hammock and lies back with a book. You tell your partner you have planned a full day of exploring this wonderful area. Your partner says they are staying in camp, but you are free to go out on your own? What is your course of action?

Scenario #13 - Accidental Death
You are in a group of six camping at Kalalau Beach on a remote section of Hawai'i's Na Pali Coast of Kaua'I, accessible by a rugged 12-mile cliff trail or by kayak. While rinsing off in the waterfall from a day of body surfing you hear someone shouting, "Does anyone know CPR?" You run down to the beach and you see a female lying face down in the sand. A person at the scene tells you the victim fell from the cliff above. A quick examination determines she is dead. There is no cell phone service or radio contact at that location. There are commercial motorized zodiacs (inflatable rafts) that speed by the beach about every hour. What is your course of action?

Scenario #14 - Bickering Couple
There is a husband and wife team that is constantly bickering during your five-day trip. It is day three and you and the rest of the group of four couples are getting tired of the couple fighting. What is your course of action?

Scenario #15 - Canyon Flash Flood
You are a leader of a youth group with five 6th graders in your charge and the six of you are hiking in the upper remote canyons of Zion Canyon National Park. The sun is still out even though the afternoon forecast is for thunderstorms in the area. You and the kids are in a narrow canyon when you hear faint sounds of thunder off in the distance but you still have sun above you.

Fifteen minutes later you start to hear a roaring sound that seems to be getting louder. You realize a flash flood is coming at you and your group. Knowing you cannot out run the flood you look for higher ground. You usher the youngsters into a side crevice that seems to be going uphill. You climb as high as you can until you reach a 12- foot high wall. You can see that the crevice keeps going up beyond the wall at a gradual angle. Since you are tall enough you know you can boost the kids up over the ledge since they cannot do it on their own. The water is rising up to your location and the children are scared. The last one in line slips back and is washed downstream. What is your course of action? Do you jump in after the one child and leave the four or stay with the four and accept the loss of the one?

Would your decision change if the one child who fell in happens to be yours? Do you jump in due to parental instincts? Do you let your child go and take care of the remaining four?

Additional Sea Kayaking Scenarios
Since I am still teaching kayaking clinics, I added some additional kayaking specific scenarios here, instead of writing an entire book just for paddlers. Even if you are not a paddler, I encourage you to continue reading the remaining scenarios because you may be able to relate many of them to non-paddling events.

Scenario #16 - Seasick Paddler
One of your group members during an eight-mile day tour gets sea sick at mile three. There are eight on the tour. The conditions are good with slight rolling seas. What is your course of action? What if this were an overuse wrist problem instead?

Scenario #17 - Surf Zone Capsize
During landing, one of your group members flips in the middle of a long surf zone. What is your course of action if:
      a) You are in your kayak outside the surf zone?
      b) You are on shore guiding the group in?
      c) You are the one who has flipped?

Scenario #18 - Sudden Fog
You are paddling alone on a six-mile day tour. Suddenly a thick fog bank overtakes you. What is your course of action?

Scenario #19 - Shark in the Area
You are just about to begin the recovery practice with your friends. A jet skier comes by to tell you a shark was spotted off the end of the pier one half mile away. He yells it out so you and the rest of the group members hear what he says. What is your course of action?

Scenario #20 - Slow Paddler
One of your friends is a very slow paddler. They are taking exceptionally long and slowing the entire group down. At the current rate of speed the group will not make the planned destination. There are six of you in the group. What is your course of action?

Scenario #21 - No Tide or Current Tables
You go on a three-day trip where there are a lot of tidal currents and you foolishly forgot to bring a tide schedule for the area, but you do have a chart. What is your course of action?

Scenario #22 - Capsize In Strong Current
You and your group of five singles misjudge the strong ebb tide and the winds. As a result, you all get pushed away from the island on which your planned campsite is located. It is near sunset and you are out in the main channel when two of the singles flip due to the rough conditions. What is your course of action?

Scenario #23 - Panicked Swimmer
One of your friends is panicking in the water after they did a wet exit. You paddle up next to them to try to calm them down. They freak out and grab you and try to climb onto your kayak. What is your course of action?

Scenario #24 - Cold and Wet Paddler
On a sunny day, one of the members of your group of four paddlers capsizes and wet exits in the cold water. They are wearing boots, polypropylene long johns, shorts, a PFD and a short sleeve cotton shirt. They are having difficulty climbing back into their boat and they keep falling back into the water even though their kayak is being is stabilized. The paddler in the water is now showing visible signs of being too cold, due to the water temperature. What is your course of action?

Scenario #25 - Flying Kayak
As you are driving down the highway you see through the rear view mirror a crash occur behind you because one of your kayaks flew off of the top of your van. You pull over and run back and see a multi-car accident with your kayak through the windshield of one of the cars. In addition, your passengers have started to follow you. What is your course of action?

CHAPTER 6

SCENARIO REVIEWS

I must state up front that these are not "THE ANSWERS." In fact there is never just one perfect way to respond to these scenarios. I will be reviewing each one using my decision-making lens. In addition, I will be including a summary of what was done and learned because some of these scenarios are based upon actual incidents.

Scenario #1 - Head Wound

On a novice backpacking trip a person stumbles off the trail and falls down a rock slope. The hiker has a head wound with the usual heavy bleeding from the scalp. Upon examination you cannot see any obvious broken bones. At first, the patient is dizzy, scared and has blurred vision. After 20 minutes, the patient is well enough to be helped back to camp. In camp the patient is still dizzy, has headaches and has disrupted vision. Your camp is two miles from the van. The nearest hospital is three hours away. It is 3pm, eight people are in the group and you are the only trip leader. What is your course of action?

Event – Head wound (bleeding, dizziness, headaches & disrupted vision)

Evaluate – Possible concussion, which is a high priority. Need to get victim to the hospital for more evaluation. There is enough daylight to get to the van. Short distance transfer is easily done. Cannot leave the group alone.

Goals –Getting victim to the hospital and see to the needs of the rest of the group.

Options – 1) Take the victim to help, which is faster. 2) Try to get help to us, which will take significantly longer. 3) Take the group as a whole. 4) Take the victim and leave the group to finish trip.

Actions – (Option 3) - Take the victim because it is the quickest option to a hospital and take the group because leaving them without a vehicle in case of another emergency is not an option. In addition, the group members are mostly novices.

Summary – This was a real trip in a side canyon of Death Valley. The nearest hospital was in Lone Pine, CA. It would be at least twice the time for advanced medical help to get to us so the decision was to transport. On this trip we had two vans and another leader so we split the group. We used a backpack frame for a seat to carry the victim to the van. The path to the van was an old road so not a high-risk transfer.

On the way out of the valley I stopped by the visitor center to have them call the hospital to let them know we were on the way and to get the doctor on call to be there when we arrived to reduce even more wait time. Result was no concussion, just needed three stitches. To add insult to injury, the sprinklers came on, in the middle of the night, in the local park where the three of us were sleeping in our bags after leaving the hospital. We drove back to the group the next day and finished the trip.

Scenario #2 - Huge Surf

You and your friends have planned today's kayaking trip for a month. The weather is beautiful but the surf is huge. You perceive some of the group members are scared but not saying anything. One of the participants is elated because he loves surf. He is very verbal about it to the point where his enthusiasm is almost catching. You know some of the group members have never dealt with surf before. What is your course of action?

Event – Huge unexpected surf at launch site.

Evaluate – Huge surf was not expected as part of this outing. Some do not have the skill level to deal with the conditions. Silence possibly due to apprehension and concern of peer pressure. There could be possible disappointment, due to expectations of a calm day. There is also enthusiasm being projected by one boater possibly adding to peer pressure.

Goals – Try to get the group to share thoughts and feelings; try to salvage the activity and do not let peer pressure push untrained paddlers into large surf conditions.

Options – 1) Speak up and share my thoughts and concerns. 2) Wait for someone else to start talking first.

Action – (Option 1) - I decided to speak first because daylight was ticking by.

Summary – I said, "I was not expecting these conditions, what about the rest of you?" Luckily my question opened a floodgate of thoughts and feelings. I was happy that one of the surf novices freely admitted they were afraid of the conditions, which prompted others to speak up. I really did not want to put anyone on the spot by suggesting that, but I would have in order to avoid a dangerous situation.

The group discussed many options, which included: having a make-shift surf class, splitting the group, finding another place to paddle and canceling the trip and go out for lunch at a favorite eatery. Going for a hike was also discussed. We decided to go out for lunch because travel time to another launch site was too long. The feeling of the group focused more on companionship then the actual paddle, which was the primary goal of the group.

We learned to have alternative locations, if possible, and to designate one in the planned group to check conditions early in the AM so we could change launch sites in advance. We also tried to set group goals for the planned trip, which would help with decisions if there were events that came up before or during the trip.

Scenario #3 - Group Dissent
You are the only leader of eight novice backpackers. The month is November and you are in a mountain top valley in

southern California at elevation 6,000 ft. You have just reached this valley after a steep five-mile uphill hike from the van. Heavy storm clouds are moving in fast. It is 3pm and a conflict develops in the group. It is cold and the rain is starting. Four members of the group want to hike back down to the van and drive or hitchhike to the nearest motel. What is your course of action?

Events – Storm moving in fast. It's cold and starting to rain. Group members want to leave location. Simultaneous events require event triage. Wet & cold take priority over group splitting up but both need action.

Evaluate – Rain or possible snow is highly likely. It will be dark long before anyone could get to the van. The steep trail gets very slippery when wet. Hiking on the steep slippery trail in the dark has very high risks of injuries and exposure. It is a novice group with some members uncomfortable and even scared.

Goals – Try to keep the group dry, warm and together; get them into shelter and fed; try to make it a positive experience.

Options – 1) Try to keep the group dry and together and spend the night where you are. 2) Hike out as a group as carefully as possible. 3) Let the four do as they please without use of the vehicle. 4) Address the concerns/needs of the four dissenters to try and change their minds. 5) Try to turn the experience into a positive one for the group.

Actions – (Options 1, 4 & 5) - Get everyone working to change their focus. Get all the tents up and all gear into the tents to stay dry. Have them don their rain gear. Get the stoves going for hot water and the evening meal. Get them into one tent (if possible) drinking hot chocolate to reduce the anxiety of the four. If you need to use two tents break up the four.

86

Summary – The gal leading the trip was an experienced backpacker and had led this trip before but not in bad weather. She decided to hike out and the group ended up in a motel for the night. Although they all got soaked, no one was injured or had symptoms of exposure.

I included my options and actions for this scenario. I believe the cause for the dissension was fear and inexperience. I have learned being warm and dry in a tent while sipping hot chocolate is very comforting. In fact, once in the tent, especially if it is storming outside, participants are not motivated to venture outside. The potential risks of fleeing in the stormy night are not worth it. I use this as a, *"What not to do,"* example in my staff training.

The hardest part is to try to keep anyone from leaving a group. Legally you cannot restrain them. However, if the positive actions mentioned above do not work I am not above convincing them it will be scarier for them to leave than to stay. One can also set an expectation before the trip that the group stays together no matter what, as a possible preventative measure.

Scenario #4 - Bike Accident
You are one of the three leaders on a bike trip. You are on the trailing bike. You come to the bottom of a steep hill on a country road and after the turn you see one of the participants wiped out in the middle of the road. You see another participant about a quarter mile away riding back towards the accident. There is no one else to be seen at the moment. The victim is lying face down on the road, has serious road rash, and is moaning, crying, and not responding well to questions. What is your course of action?

Events – Bike accident with injured person lying in the middle of the road.

Evaluate – Victim is in a potentially dangerous location. The victim is breathing because they are making noise. One direction has a curve and the other is a straight, flat road. I have one person to help me. The biker was probably moving fast when they hit the pavement.

Goals – Try to keep any of us from getting run over by a passing vehicle; I need to assess the injuries to see if they can be moved off of the road; if there are serious injuries, stabilize the victim until emergency personnel arrive; try to contact emergency services and the other leaders.

Options – 1) Pull them off of the road and then assess. 2) Assess to see if they can be moved, but be ready to move them should an approaching car fail to slow down. 3) Send the other biker up the curve to slow approaching vehicles or send them to tell the other leaders. 4) Wave down a passing car and ask them to call for help at the nearest phone or ask them to help slow traffic or contact the other leaders.

Actions – (Options 2 & 3) - I ask the second biker to go up the curve to slow vehicles and return to me if he or she hears the sound of the whistle I carry. I assess the victim to see if they can be moved. If they can, then the immediate danger is alleviated. If not, then we need to secure the area as best we can, with one eye on the possibility of pulling the victim off the road to keep them from being run over. If we do pull them away, we make every effort to move them as a unit to reduce the chance of additional injury.

Summary – This was a made up scenario for bike leaders and it was prior to cell phones and inexpensive radios. I wanted the staff to avoid the number one mistake made by first aiders, which is moving the victim or moving them too much and think of ways to secure the area if possible. We also trained them the best way to move someone if it was absolutely necessary.

We always had a trailing sag wagon that would have caught up to the accident, but it did not consistently follow the last biker. We did not want to slow normal traffic. The sag wagon would stop and go. The wagon gave us options for getting help and getting to other leaders.

In hindsight, we should have required all bike leaders carry at least four road flares for such an emergency. It seems obvious now, but none of us thought of carrying flares back then.

Scenario #5 - Cave Kayaking

You and two others are leading a kayak tour around one of the Channel Islands off of the California coast. As the head guide for the day you are checking out the interior of a sea cave before you let the group enter. While in the cave alone, a big set of swells roll in and you find yourself being bashed into the back wall of the cave. As a result of the impact you get injured; are knocked out of your kayak and it is too painful for you to call for help. What is your course of action?

Events – In a sea cave alone, injured, in pain, which prohibits calling out or moving. Out of my kayak and in the water.

Evaluate – Right now I cannot do anything to help myself due to the pain. I am in the water but I am dressed for immersion. I am wearing a PFD (floatation device) and a helmet. I do not feel any head or neck injuries. I do have a whistle on my PFD.

Goals – Get out of the cave before another set of waves come in; deal with my injuries and try and signal for help.

Options – 1) Float in the cave and wait for help. 2) Try to slowly swim out. 3) Blow the whistle, if it not too painful.

Actions – (Options 2 & 3) - Try to blow the whistle and slowly swim out because the sooner I am out of the cave the less likely I will get pounded should there be more waves.

Summary – We always assess the wave patterns before entering any sea caves. The seas were relatively calm so I went in to scout this cave when a rogue set of waves came in. The rear chamber had a nice gravel beach in the back where I could sit and watch the waves break in front of me on the shore. Sunlight beamed down through an opening in the ceiling, which was an added bonus, because most sea caves are almost pitch black inside. Instead of waiting on the shore I tried to paddle into the waves because the waves triggered a *trained response*. In this case it was the wrong response. I got knocked off my sit-on-top kayak at least three times as I kept trying to paddle into the waves. Again, it was my default response to waves. Eventually the waves stopped and I was able to paddle out, uninjured.

This event was the reason we established protocols for dealing with being caught in sea caves which include: how and when to send in help, how to survive inside the cave with incoming waves and signaling if rogue waves appear.

Scenario #6 - Trip Location Change
You decide to finally do that solo back county trip. You told your significant other your plans and when you would be home. When you get to the trailhead you find the route you want to take appears too risky due to posted bear attack signs. You decide to drive to another location a few hours away. There is no cell phone service at either location. While on your trip you get injured and cannot make your way back to the car. What is your course of action?

Events – Injured in the backcountry, cannot get out on your own and nobody knows where you are because you moved locations.

Evaluate – I know there is no way I can get out on my own, which means I am here until help arrives.

Goals – Stay warm, dry, hydrated and fed; I need to send some type(s) of signal while I wait for help.

Options – 1) Do what I can to stay warm, dry, hydrated and fed. 2) Regularly blow on my whistle and use my mirror to flash sunlight at any passing planes. 3) Ration my supplies.

Actions – (Options 1, 2 & 3) - I would do what I can to stay warm, dry, hydrated and fed. Regularly blow on my whistle.

Use my mirror to flash sunlight at any passing planes. Ration my supplies.

Summary – I use this scenario to discuss the plans we leave with others that have our itinerary and when they should call authorities. In kayaking we call it a float plan. It also gives us the opportunity to discuss satellite locator beacons and satellite phones.

When planning a trip, especially a solo one, you should have alternative locations on your float plan, which is being proactive. In this case this hiker could have left a note at the original trailhead as to their new plan. In hindsight that extra thirty-minute drive to the pay phone would have been worth it. If your trailhead area had three different trails leave a note in your visor, which route you took. Your float plan has your car info on it so search & rescue may try to gain access to your locked car to get more info.

As for satellite locator beacons they are a great last resort. My only objection to them is if a person depends on them instead of being well trained. Yes, emergencies do happen, but to do foolish things thinking you can just press a button and help will arrive is being irresponsible. Rescuers may be risking their lives coming to help you. I should mention, in a steep canyon or in high mountain country the signal may get blocked or deflected...often becoming a ghost signal not giving your true location.

Leave a float plan with alternatives. Let your contact know if there are changes. Call your contact when you get out. When search and rescue is called out they start looking where you said you would be.

Scenario #7 - Equipment Failure
While leading a backpacking trip into the mountains you and your fellow leader discover that the two stoves you brought along are not working. You brought food that has to be cooked. Fires are strictly prohibited with a $5,000 fine. The ranger told you they are enforcing the "No Fire" restriction

with full penalty because last month they lost 50,000 acres of original growth trees and the fire danger is still high. There are 12 very hungry backpackers who have hiked ten miles up to 10,000 ft. and the sun is setting. What is your course of action?

Event – The stoves are not working.

Evaluate – It is late in the day, you have meals that need to be cooked, the hikers are hungry and fires are prohibited.

Goals – Get the stoves working and feed the hikers.

Options – 1) Try to fix the stoves with your repair kit. 2) Eat the food uncooked. 3) Soak the uncooked food to make it more palatable or put the food and water in a zip lock bag and use body heat to slightly warm it. 4) Make a very small, well-protected fire to cook the food. 5) Save the food that has to be cooked for tomorrow and use the most edible foods for tonight. 6) Hike out to get different food or a working stove or end the trip. 7) Ask the group what they prefer doing regarding the meals.

Actions – (Options 1, 5 & 7) - Try and fix the stove. If you can, save the food that has to be cooked for tomorrow and use the most edible foods for tonight. Ask the group what they prefer doing regarding the meals. I would not start a fire.

Summary – I use this for my staff to be proactive with respect to their equipment and meal planning. Standard operating procedure (SOP) for our program was to check all stoves before leaving campus. All broken equipment should be placed on the "needs repair" shelf after a trip if it is not functioning. We also had an equipment manager who checked all equipment before the trip went out while knowing it is the responsibility of the trip leaders to do so. This gave us a double check. All staff were trained to fix the stoves and other equipment they had along. Personally I make sure all my equipment is put away for future use in working condition and checked again before the trip. On a trip to Seattle in the early 1980's I spent hours with the stove guru at REI learning how to fix stoves.

As for food, we tried to bring food that could be eaten cold as is or at least soaked in water. The truth is there are very few food items you could not eat if you were really hungry. The big difference is the taste and palatability. If you eat uncooked freeze-dried food and drink water it will hydrate in your stomach to some degree. I would prefer option 3 instead of rehydrating in my stomach. If water is scarce, eating too much or eating dehydrated foods forces your body to use too much of it's own water, which can cause you to become dehydrated.

Respect fire bans; being a little hungry is insignificant to the risk to lives, the loss of homes, the loss of trees and animals due to uncontrolled fires.

Scenario #8 - Behind Schedule
You are leading a beginner's canoe trip and the group is extremely slow. Most of the canoes are not maintaining a straight course. It takes you 5 hours to get to a lunch spot that normally takes 2 hours. Wind and current are adding to the difficulty of the canoeists. An hour after a very late lunch break you realize you will not reach your intended camp, with the hot springs, until well after dark. The air temperature is getting colder. It is November, you are in the Arizona/Nevada desert area and you are in a river canyon. What is your course of action?

Event –Behind schedule.

Evaluate – The group's pace is slow due to wind and current. You will not make the planned destination before dark, if at all. The group is tired and pushing too much increases risks. Weather conditions not an issue at this time, but temperatures are going down. There are many campsites along the route.

Goals – Get the group off the water before injuries, major frustration, undue fatigue and/or exposure ensues.

Options – 1) Find the nearest campsite. 2) Take a break and go for a site farther up stream. 3) Push the group to the planned campsite because you promised them the hot springs tonight.

Actions – (Option 1) - Find the nearest campsite because we are self-contained and this trip is supposed to be enjoyable. There are numerous adequate sites all along the river. The hot springs will be there tomorrow when you continue up river.

Summary – This is a great example of where sticking to the itinerary becomes a detriment. The leaders of this lower Colorado canoe trip had an epiphany as a result. They realized that by being self contained they can camp anywhere that had enough space and that talking so much about the hot springs was putting self-imposed pressure on them in addition to the expectations they were setting within the group.

They stopped at the first available camp and had a wonderful night. There was some disappointment, but the rest and the food were a good consolation to the hot springs. The group also knew they would get to the springs the next day.
The two important lessons to be learned from this are: one, be careful in how you set expectations; and two, keep your itinerary flexible. When you are self-contained, anywhere you stop is fine. I like to use the line from the movie *The Adventures of Buckaroo Banzai Across the 8th Dimension*, "No matter where you go, there you are."

Scenario #9 - Snow Slope
You and your two friends have been trying to get out for a one-day cross-country ski trip for the last month. The weekdays have been sunny, but each weekend there were heavy snowstorms so you kept postponing the trip. Finally the weather pattern changed and you have a favorable

forecast. The weather turned out to be great. The three of you have been having a great day skiing in the backcountry. As all of you ski across an open slope, discussing the Seahawks game, you hear a strange sound as you feel the snow underneath your skis settle. What is your course of action?

Event – The snow slope settled underneath the three of you.

Evaluate – The three of you are on a slope that settled, the possibility of an avalanche is high. Your present location is risky.

Goals – To get off the exposed slope before it slides. Separate the three of you with the hopes of having at least one of you to search if the slope does give way. Be ready to swim to the top of the slide if you are caught in an avalanche.

Options – 1) Head back the way you came one at a time. Since the slope didn't slide on the way in you have better odds in that direction. 2) All head back together at once to get off the slope as quickly as possible. 3) Continue forward one at a time. 4) Continue forward all at once. 5) Loosen pack and remove pole straps to easily get rid of them in case of slide.

Actions – (Options 1 & 5) - I would head back one at a time and be ready to get rid of my pack & poles should a slide occur. Try to find a protected area, possible below some rocks and evaluate your options.

Summary – If you are a backcountry skier I highly recommend an avalanche safety course. In this scenario the weather conditions reported for the prior month would be a red flag if you were trained properly. The three of you should not have been close together. Crossing suspect slopes should be done one at a time so the others could help. Wearing and knowing how to use avalanche beacons is a must for backcountry skiers. This is another, "*What not to do,*" scenario.

Scenario #10 - Emergency Stop

You are driving your family to a long anticipated vacation on the water. You're cruising at the speed limit (60 mph) and you are towing boats on a trailer. Up ahead you see a minivan parked on the side of this two-lane road, which has a very wide shoulder. The passengers are out of the van and someone is changing a flat tire. There is traffic coming in the opposite direction. Just as you get close to the van a dog darts out right in front of your vehicle. What is your course of action?

Event - Dog runs out in front of your vehicle while you are towing a trailer with boats.

Evaluate – I need to react immediately, because I may kill the dog. I am going 60 mph. Cars are coming in the other direction.

Goals – Try not to kill the dog; maintain the well-being of my family, myself and others in the area in that order.

Options – 1) Slam on the brakes to avoid hitting the dog, which will cause my vehicle to skid and the trailer jackknife to one side or the other. 2) Slow as quickly as possible while under control and pull over when acceptable and deal with hitting the dog. 3) Swerve, into oncoming traffic or the parked van, to avoid the dog.

Actions – (Option 2) - Slow as quickly as possible while under control and pull over when acceptable and deal with hitting the dog. I cannot swerve because of oncoming traffic. I do not slam on the brakes because I know I will lose control of the vehicle and trailer.

Summary – This scenario is designed to force you to examine and prioritize your values. The gut reaction of many drivers is to slam on the brakes, which will not keep you from hitting the dog. In addition, the skidding vehicle with a trailer sliding out to the side could hit the van on the side of the road along with the family or slide into oncoming traffic.

In case you didn't know, the average stopping distance at 60 mph (without a trailer) is 240 feet, which, to give you some perspective, is 80 yards on a football field. The first 60 feet is just reaction time. You travel 80 feet/sec at that speed, which means you will probably hit the dog before you even get to the brake.

You do not have the luxury of time to analyze all of this when a split second decision needs to be made. Before you get behind the wheel of a vehicle you need to know if you value an animal's life more than a human's. Is one life valued more than two or more? Is your family a greater priority to you than strangers? I ask these questions because how would you react if a little girl ran out after the dog?

I have trained my staff to slow as quickly as possible while under control and then go back and deal with the results. This is not easy, but it is necessary because we usually have to drive to get to our adventures.

Scenario #11 - No Sleeping Bag
You and two friends are packing your backpacks at the trailhead for a three-day outing. You suddenly realize you left your sleeping bag sitting in your garage. You are 5 hours from home and there is only one car. What is your course of action?

Event – Discover you have no sleeping bag while at trailhead.

Evaluate – Nighttime temperatures necessitate a bag. Too long to drive home and get the bag. Only have one car.

Goals – Do the trip and stay warm at night.

Options – 1) Wear extra clothes at night and sleep by a fire. 2) Zip two bags together to see if the three of you can fit. 3) See if there were any hikers in the parking lot with an extra bag they would be willing to lend you. 4) Check to see if there is a store close enough to buy a bag. 5) Develop a way the two bags could cover the three of you. 6) Sit in the car until your two friends come back from their trip. 7) Cancel the trip and go home.

Action – (Option 5) - You and your friends found a way the two bags could cover the three of you.

Summary – There have been a few times when sleeping bags were forgotten during our program trips. Connecting like zippered bags together and using them as a blanket, was the *"go to"* option. This is when you need to use your ingenuity if you do not want to leave someone behind. I had one staff member who stayed awake all night doing jumping jacks to warm up on his solo-kayaking trip. He didn't realize he didn't put the bag into the kayak until he unpacked.

As a result of bags being forgotten, we did a sleeping bag check before the vans left the campus. We figure the bag was essential for a good night's sleep.

If extreme cold temperatures are forecasted it would require greater evaluation. It may mean someone gets left behind or the trip is cancelled. Leaving the others without a vehicle if you go to a hotel can be risky if they had to leave in an emergency.

Having a thorough checklist minimizes your chance of leaving something behind. I use a double check system. First check is when I put it in the pile. The second check is when it is in the vehicle. See *Appendix 1 on Pack Lists*.

Scenario #12 - Different Agendas
You and your significant other are on your one-week summer vacation. You have been telling your partner about this location for the past few years and you are finally here. You wake up early and are rearing to get up and explore the area, but your partner seems to be lounging in the tent. To your surprise, after a late breakfast, your partner sets up a hammock and lies back with a book. You tell your partner you have planned a full day of exploring this wonderful area.

Your partner says they are staying in camp, but you are free to go out on your own? What is your course of action?

Event – You are ready to go and your partner isn't going.

Evaluate – You realize you have different agendas. You feel this is a high priority because of your expectations. You are feeling upset/disappointed.

Goal – You want your partner to go with you to share the experience.

Options – 1) Go alone feeling disappointed. 2) Stay in camp with my partner and be disappointed. 3) Try to convince them to go. 4) Find out why they don't want to go. 5) Try to find a win-win alternative.

Actions – (Options 4 & 5) - Find out why they don't want to go. Try to find a win-win alternative.

Summary – If there is more than one person on a trip there will be different expectations and different agendas. Unfortunately some or many of these differences come out on the trip, which can lead to disappointment, bad feelings, arguing and resentment. Just because you were talking about this trip for years it doesn't mean your partner had the same ideas as you as to the itinerary of the trip. To avoid and/or minimize these issues, those on the trip should clarify their expectations and share it with the others.

I learned this the hard way when my girlfriend decided to go back to the camp to lie in a hammock and read a book instead of paddling to see a pod of orcas. I was upset because I felt she could read a book at home. I was thinking you don't get a chance to see orcas everyday. Later in camp I expressed my thoughts. Her reply was very enlightening. She asked, "Do you have any idea what a luxury it is for me to lay back in these beautiful surroundings and read a book after being stuck in my office week after week and month after month?" We had a great discussion after that.

The experience led to a talk we did a number of times at kayak symposia called, "He kayaks; She kayaks." It was a discussion of how we saw the trip from our own perspectives. The talks, mostly attended by couples, saw heads constantly shaking up and down throughout the presentations because they related to our experiences and the differences raised.

I think it is a good idea to ask the participants what they would like to get out of the trip before you take off. It can be done as part of the introductions if it is a new group. If it is friends, it is still good to find out each other's expectations or desires.

Scenario #13 - Accidental Death
You are in a group of six camping at Kalalau Beach on a remote section of Hawai'i's Na Pali Coast of Kaua'I, accessible by a rugged 12-mile cliff trail or by kayak. While rinsing off in the waterfall from a day of body surfing you hear someone shouting, "Does anyone know CPR?" You run down to the beach and you see a female lying face down in the sand. A person at the scene tells you the victim fell from the cliff above. A quick examination determines she is dead. There is no cell phone service or radio contact at that location. There are commercial motorized zodiacs (inflatable rafts) that speed by the beach about every hour. What is your course of action?

Event – Dead female on the beach

Evaluate – No rush but something needs to be done beyond covering the body.

Goals – Contact the authorities. Find out if anyone knows the girl. Keep my group and others away out of respect and try to address emotional issues of those involved.

Options – 1) Swim out and flag down the next passing zodiac to tell them to send in search and rescue to retrieve the body. 2) Find out more about the girl. 3) Have someone keep others away. 4) Open dialog with my group about the event.

Actions – In this case, all of the options listed.

Summary – This happened during one of my Kaua'i kayaking trips. I took the actions I listed above. There was a lot more I had to deal with as a result of this tragic death in a paradise setting. The girl was part of a large school group. The dead girl's group was in varying states of emotional shock. Don (my co-leader) and I had to see to it the group ate and stayed hydrated. We worked with the group's leader to assist in any way we could. A helicopter arrived to retrieve the body about three to four hours after I had flagged down the zodiac.

We also had to deal with our group, who was affected even though they did not see the body. We did a lot of talking that night and the next few days to help alleviate some of the emotions that resulted from the death.

That night Don suggested we have my friend John, who lands a zodiac each morning at our beach, call our boss to tell him about the death and that it was NOT in our group. This was in case this hit the news, which it did. When we got back to the university my boss thanked us for the heads up. The news headlines read, "Girl from a California College fell to her death on Kaua'i." This is a perfect example of you knowing you are OK, but others need to hear it too.

Scenario #14 - Bickering Couple
There is a husband and wife team that is constantly bickering during your five-day trip. It is day three and you and the rest of the group of four couples are getting tired of the couple fighting. What is your course of action?

Event – Group frustration due to one couple constantly arguing.

Evaluate – Group frustration is high and needs immediate resolution. Needs a tactful resolution.

Goal – Have the arguing stop.

Options – 1) Have one spokesperson from the group speak with the couple. 2) Have the group speak with the couple. 3) Speak to the couple individually.

Action - (Option 1) - Have one spokesperson from the group speak with the couple, because it is better to get one clear message rather than a bunch of them, from the group.

Summary – It is always difficult to deal with personal matters amongst friends. Being direct, but sensitive, is the best approach. Your goal is to have the fighting stop for the rest of the trip. The biggest danger is getting involved in their dispute. You are not there to resolve the issue. You do not take sides. You especially don't want the group involved and taking sides. Ask the couple to call a truce for the rest of the trip.

In this example, I would have approached the couple at the end of the first day instead of waiting three days. Knowing me I probably would have yelled aloud, in the first hour, a joking comment like, "Keep it down you're ruining my wilderness experience." If it didn't stop it, it would at least put the couple on notice that others are being affected by their bickering.

Scenario #15 - Canyon Flash Flood
You are a leader of a youth group with five 6th graders in your charge and the six of you are hiking in the upper remote canyons of Zion Canyon National Park. The sun is still out even though the afternoon forecast is for thunderstorms in the area. You and the kids are in a narrow canyon when you hear faint sounds of thunder off in the distance but you still have sun above you.

Fifteen minutes later you start to hear a roaring sound that seems to be getting louder. You realize a flash flood is coming at you and your group. Knowing you cannot out run the flood you look for higher ground. You usher the youngsters into a side crevice that seems to be going uphill. You climb as high as you can until you reach a 12- foot high wall. You can see that the crevice keeps going up beyond the wall at a gradual angle. Since you are tall enough you know you can boost the kids up over the ledge since they cannot do it on their own. The water is rising up to your location and the children are scared. The last one in line slips back and is washed downstream. What is your course of action? Do you jump in after the one child and leave the four or stay with the four and accept the loss of the one?

Would your decision change if the one child who fell in happens to be yours? Do you jump in due to parental instincts? Do you let your child go and take care of the remaining four?

Events – Flash flood in a canyon. Child swept away.

Evaluate – One child is gone and I have four more still in danger requiring immediate action.

Goal – Save as many as I can.

Options – 1) Go after the one, with the hopes the others will survive on their own, in their present location. 2) Help the remainder of the group to higher ground and stay with them. 3) Help the group to higher ground and then go after the one who was washed away.

Actions – (Option 2) - Help the remaining children to higher ground and stay with them. Get to outside help as quickly as possible to start a search for the missing child.

Summary – This is one of those nightmare scenarios that should never have happened. Hiking in canyons or desert ravines when there are forecasts for thunderstorms, is not only negligent, it is criminal. Even if it is not raining on you, the flood can come from heavy rains miles away. Once the rains flood a ravine or canyon it will continue downstream, picking up debris along the way.

If you are hiking in these areas you should be regularly checking for escape routes if there is any suspect of rain in the distance.

If I did end up in this scenario I would save the four over the one. I believe I would do the same even if the one were my child. Keep in mind I am saying this not as a parent and from the comfort of my home. I strongly believe the four lives are more important than one.

There is another point to consider, which is the wisdom of leading a group that has one or more of your children in it. Many outings in the scouting programs have parents leading the group. I am not criticizing the scouting program. They do fantastic work. I raise the issue because other parents are counting on you as the leader to bring their kids back in one piece. I believe this issue needs to be reviewed and discussed by parent trip leaders. These leaders need to examine their values in advance. I have read too many accounts of parents jumping into a whitewater river after their child fell in with the hopes of saving them only to drown in the process. It was a gut instinct that drove them.

When you have the responsibility of a number of lives, knowing how you should act in advance is important if a choice needs to be made. This is when the proactive DMP with postponed actions needs to be explored.

Overall Summary
You have just read my responses to the above scenarios. I am willing to bet there were many similarities and differences in how you responded. I also acknowledge if more details were given, it would have reduced some of the assumptions you had to make when answering.

The purpose in answering these scenarios is two-fold. First, it lets you practice your own DMP, which allows you to get more clarity into your decision-making lens-factors. Second, and more importantly, there are lessons to be learned from the experience of others. You are gaining collective experience, without having to live through the actual event, in the hope of avoiding similar situations in the future. If however, you cannot avoid the event, then maybe you will be better equipped to deal with it because you have already gone through the process in a practice setting.

Additional Sea Kayaking Scenarios
Even if you decided not to respond to these kayak specific scenarios listed in the previous chapter, I encourage you to read through my responses because some of the lessons learned might be helpful to you in other situations that do not involve kayaking.

Scenario #16 - Seasick Paddler
One of your group members during an eight-mile day tour gets seasick at mile three. There are eight on the tour. The conditions are good with slight rolling seas. What is your course of action? What if this were an overuse wrist problem instead?

Event – Seasick paddler

Evaluate – Paddler feeling nauseous and dizzy. There are regular rolling seas. It is three miles to the launching area and the cars. It is two miles to the next landing with road access, but the entire route in either direction has easy beach landings.

Goals – To get the sick paddler off of the water; try to reduce nausea; keep them upright and be prepared for vomiting.

Options – 1) Keep the sick paddler moving while watching the horizon line hoping the symptoms will subside. 2) Have the sick kayaker paddle to shore as soon as possible. 3) Tow the sick paddler to shore with a second boater stabilizing the

105

ailing kayaker's boat. 4) Discuss protocols for vomiting while sitting in a kayak.

Actions – (Options 3 & 4) - Discuss protocols for vomiting while sitting in a kayak, with the sick boater, and then tow them to shore with a second boater stabilizing the ailing kayaker's boat.

Summary – After assisting dozens of seasick paddlers I have learned 95% of the time they are done for the day once they feel nausea and dizziness. The greatest concern is keeping them from flipping over and possibly inhaling water. When a person throws up their normal breathing pattern is disrupted. Imagine being upside down while vomiting. You may uncontrollably inhale while under the water. Therefore keeping the paddler from capsizing is important.

I instruct nauseous paddlers to vomit straight down on their spray skirts instead of leaning over the side so they don't capsize if they are unattended. After a seasick person vomits there is a short window of relief. That window varies in time. This brief time could be used to paddle as quickly as possible to a road access. Fast paddling many times prolongs the relief window. However, when the symptoms return they come back much worse. Fluid replacement is essential after being sick for two reasons; addressing dehydration and having some contents in your tummy if you get sick again. It is better than dry heaves.

Getting the paddler off the water quickly minimizes their discomfort. Severe seasickness can be debilitating. Once they are on solid ground the symptoms will begin to lessen. While on the beach, the exit options for the sick paddler, needs to be discussed. They eventually have to get back to their car. They can either paddle two miles or three miles. The three miles gets them right to their car. The two miles gets them to a road access, which can be a waiting spot until the vehicles are shuttled. If you choose to paddle, be ready to tow them with a second boater supporting the kayak being towed.

Another option is the paddler walks along the beach back to the put-in or the nearest road access, if the beach route allows it. Their empty kayak can be towed back to their car.

Scenario #17 - Surf Zone Capsize
During landing, one of your group members flips in the middle of a long surf zone. What is your course of action if:
a) You are in your kayak outside the surf zone?
b) You are on shore guiding the group in?
c) You are the one who has flipped?

Event
a) A group member flips in the surf zone.
b) A group member flips in the surf zone.
c) My kayak capsized in the middle of the surf zone.

Evaluate
a) They are out of their kayak, which is now a few feet away from them. They flashed the OK sign with one arm, while holding their paddle in the other. Their kayak is being pushed to shore by the waves faster than they are swimming. My kayak could be a danger to them if I enter the surf zone.

b) They are out of their kayak, which is now a few feet away from them. They flashed the OK sign with one arm, while holding their paddle in the other. Their kayak is being pushed to shore by the waves faster than they are swimming.

c) I am out of my kayak. I signaled the OK sign with one arm to let the others know I am fine, while still holding my paddle. I couldn't hold on to my kayak, which is now a few feet away from me.

Goals
a) Get all paddlers to shore with minimal to no injury. Not cause injury to others.

b) Get all paddlers to shore with minimal to no injury. Not cause injury to others.

c) Get me and my kayak to shore.

Options

a) 1- Stay with the rest of the paddlers, outside of the surf zone, and direct them in once the zone is cleared of the swimmer. 2- Go into the zone to help the swimmer.

b) 1- Wait for the paddler to swim to shore. 2- Retrieve their kayak if it gets washed ashore by the continuous waves. 3- Swim out to help them. 4- Paddle out to help them.

c) 1- Try to get to my kayak and do a self-recovery and then paddle to shore. 2- Do a paddle swim to shore and let the waves push my kayak to shore. 3- Signal for help if I feel I need it.

Actions

a) (Option 1) - I stay with the others because that is my designated job. If I go into the surf zone, with my kayak, I can be a significant danger to the swimmer if I am pushed by a wave towards them.

b) (Option 1) - I will wait for the paddler to swim to shore. Retrieve their kayak if it gets washed ashore by the continuous waves. Since they gave the OK signal and have their paddle they can do a paddle swim to shore. I will be ready to go in to help them if they begin waving or it appears they need assistance.

c) (Option 2) - I decided to do a paddle swim to shore and let the waves push my kayak to shore. There was not enough time to get to my kayak before the next wave pushed it even farther from me. In addition, the wave frequency was too short to allow the self-recovery techniques I am capable of performing.

Summary
There should be designated jobs and protocols in place when doing group launchings and landings through surf zones. Since it is rare to do successful capsize recoveries in the zone, due to the time between waves, the best option is to have the capsized paddler swim in with their paddle and let the waves take the boat in. Some daring paddlers prefer to hold onto their kayak and get pulled in by the kayak as the waves do the work. This option can be risky depending on your technique and the size of the waves, so it is not recommended.

It is common to have the paddler in the staging area, outside of the zone, not enter the area of breaking waves for rescues. Since anything in the zone gets washed to shore anyway, it is only a matter of time before the paddler and kayak are on land. Their job is to organize the group when they paddle out. They set the landing order after the lead paddler goes to shore to start the landing process.

The lead paddler on shore is the one in charge of the entire landing and launching operation. They choose the paddler for the staging area, they pick the order for launching and are there to launch and land the kayakers. If someone capsizes in the zone the lead will designate a rescue swimmer or boater to help, while they stay and supervise the entire process.

Scenario #18 - Sudden Fog
You are paddling alone on a six-mile day tour. Suddenly a thick fog bank overtakes you. What is your course of action?

Event – Overtaken by fog.

Evaluate – No visibility and not exactly sure which way to go.

Goal – Get back to shore.

Options – 1) Paddle in the direction I think is correct. 2) Regularly blow my whistle, hoping to hear a response. 3) Listen intently for any recognizable sounds.

Actions – Use all options. Paddle in the direction I think is correct. Regularly blow on my whistle, hoping to hear a response. Listen intently for any recognizable sounds.

Summary – A paddler who got stuck in the fog when he was a novice shared this story with me. He said it was pure luck he even got to shore. Then he walked his kayak along the shoreline, in the shallows, until he got to a road access. It was about a mile walk.

It was obvious he was inexperienced because this should never happen. As long as you are regularly scanning your surroundings fog cannot sneak up on you. When you see fog in the distance it is time to paddle toward your take-out while getting your compass bearing at the same time.

On bodies of water where fog is a possibility, your standard equipment should be a deck-mounted compass or, at the very least, a handheld one so you can take your necessary readings while you still have visibility. If you carry a GPS, and know how to use it, you can easily navigate in the fog. If you are being proactive, you can plot and record the necessary course headings before you even get on the water in the event visibility becomes impaired.

The difficulty when paddling in fog, without a compass, is trying to maintain a straight course. I have yet to meet a kayaker who can paddle in a straight line with their eyes closed. Most of them go off course in the first 20 strokes.

If you pay attention to your surroundings, you may be able to determine a general direction from shadows, currents and swell direction.

Scenario #19 - Shark in the Area

You are just about to begin the recovery practice with your friends. A jet skier comes by to tell you a shark was spotted off the end of the pier one half mile away. He yells it out so you and the rest of the group members hear what he says. What is your course of action?

Event – Shark sighting in your area.

Evaluate – Potential for shark attack has increased for recovery practice.

Goals – Not to get attacked and practice recoveries.

Options – 1) Head back to shore. 2) Practice recoveries as planned and ignore the sighting. 3) Let individuals decide for themselves.   4) Go for a paddle instead.

Actions – (Option 3) - Let individuals decide for themselves. Since this is a group of friends, challenge by choice is an important consideration.

Summary – I was observing an instructor trainee on his final practicum. We were already practicing capsize recoveries. After the jet skier left, the trainee looked at me with questioning eyes. I said, "It is your class, you make the call." He paddled over, for a sidebar, and said he was not comfortable making this decision. After a short discussion he asked if I would take over the class. He did indicate if I weren't there he would take everyone back to shore.

Seeing this as a great teaching moment, I asked the class, "What should we do?" We had a great discussion on risk, challenge by choice and the shark attack statistics for the south coast of California. Since it was a formal class I had to consider safety and liability above the desires of the group. We eventually headed to shore without anyone else getting into the water. The thought that made the decision an easy one was, "How could I justify allowing my students to get into the water after being told of a shark sighting in the immediate area?" This was a prime example of future hindsight.

Aside from safety and liability concerns, I perceived there were ego and peer pressure issues lurking about among the students. It could see it in their body language, facial expressions, their dialog and hesitations. When I said I could not allow them to continue getting in the water and we needed to head in, I felt a huge silent sigh of relief as we turned towards shore.

I find it ironic that just a hundred yards from our teaching location is a favorite surfing location called Campus Point (UCSB Campus) in Southern California. There were surfers on their boards while our class was going on. Since this is part of the Pacific Ocean, a wide variety of sharks and other creatures are always in the water. The potential for a shark attack is always there. We cannot accurately calculate if the actual risk increased due to the news of the sighting. We don't know what kind of shark was seen or its size. What does matter is the perceived risk did change. The decision to end the class was made putting a priority on the perception, because part of program's mission-statement includes fun. Being terrified and possibly humiliated, for not getting in the water, is not part of our program's values.

Scenario #20 - Slow Paddler
One of your friends is a very slow paddler. They are taking exceptionally long and slowing the entire group down. At the current rate of speed the group will not make the planned destination. There are six of you in the group. What is your course of action?

Event – Behind schedule due to slow paddler.

Evaluate – Cannot make the planned destination unless we increase the pace. The slow paddler cannot paddle any faster.

Goals – Keep the group together; enjoy the trip; be off the water with enough daylight to set up camp and make dinner.

Options – 1) Have the strongest paddler tow the slower paddler to get to the planned destination, satisfying the stated time concerns. 2) Use your current pace to determine viable alternative campsites that meet your time concerns.

Actions – (Option 2) - Pick a new campsite to meet your time concerns. Your scheduled destination is just a plan. I once heard someone say, "If you want to make God laugh, make a plan." Your other goals are keeping the group together and having fun. You can do all of that at another campsite. The feelings of the slow paddler, with respect to being towed, needs to be considered. Is the possible embarrassment worth getting to the planned camp?

Summary – Keeping paddlers together is one of the greatest challenges on group trips. I once wrote an article for Sea Kayaker Magazine (which is now defunct) called *Team Towing*. It discusses the stigma and the ways a towrope can keep a group together. The article can be found on my website.

If the slow paddler and the strong paddlers are up for the towing option, then you are back on track. If not, then choosing an alternative campsite is your only option, given your stated goals. These trips are meant to be fun. This is yet another reason why itineraries need to be flexible. Here are some proactive approaches to the slow paddler dilemma:

- Only go with paddlers who can maintain a certain pace. Make it part of the trip announcement.
- If there is a tandem kayak along, have the slower paddler move into the tandem if the substitute can paddle at the needed pace and are willing to do so.
- Prior to the trip, make it clear towropes will be used to help maintain the needed group pace to meet the scheduled itinerary.

- Be ready with alternative campsites all along your route. Aside from a slow paddler, there are numerous reasons that can affect the group's pace, such as: illness, injury or environmental conditions.

Scenario #21 - No Tide or Current Tables
You go on a three-day trip where there are a lot of tidal currents and you foolishly forgot to bring a tide or current schedule for the area, but you do have a chart. What is your course of action?

Event – No tide or current tables

Evaluate – My chart tells me the current directions, but I do not know when they change or their strength.

Goals– Go on my trip and use the currents to my advantage when applicable.

Options – 1) Try to find new tables near my present location. There must be a fishing boat nearby with that info. 2) Just go on the planned trip and hope the current is going with me instead of against me. 3) Try to judge the tides by the most recent high water lines.

Actions – (Options 1, 2 & 3) - I will try to find some tables, as I get ready to launch. In addition, I will check the water lines to see if the tide is coming in or going out. Once I know the high tide time, I know low tide will be approximately 6 hours later (one of the many reasons I always have a watch). I can check my chart and see the current directions for ebbing and flooding. If I can figure out the tidal flow before I leave, I can wait to launch if waiting is in my favor.

Summary – In this case the paddler was unprepared due to a packing mistake. Knowing this can happen to anyone, it would be wise to memorize the first day's tidal information before you leave the house. Using the currents to your advantage is just wise trip planning.

Hopefully the days you have chosen and your itinerary will let you go with the flow. Even though I don't remember the exact times of the current tables, I remember the general timing after my planning is complete. As an example: I expect to launch at 10 AM, paddle against the current an hour, then have the current with me to camp. Even if I forget my tables, I know the plan I researched at home.

Since most people have smart phones, there are numerous tidal apps available. If you do not have cell service, you can look for a hot spot. If you are launching from a marina there will be plenty of tidal information there and possible free wifi connections. You can do an online search for the *Rule of 12ths* if you want to know more about estimating tidal flow.

Scenario #22 - Capsize In Strong Current
You and your group of five singles misjudge the strong ebb tide and the winds. As a result, you all get pushed away from the island on which your planned campsite is located. It is near sunset and you are out in the main channel when two of the singles flip due to the rough conditions. What is your course of action?

Event – Two kayaks have capsized. Tidal flow is moving you away from your planned destination.

Evaluate – Two paddlers in the water. Sunset is approaching. Tidal flow is controlling your location.

Goals– Get the swimmers back in their kayaks ready to paddle; keep the group together and try to get to a campsite before dark.

Options – 1) Get the paddlers into their kayaks immediately to reduce exposure time. 2) Try to find the nearest camping area with the least amount of resistance to the flow. 3) Fight the current to get back to your planned campsite.

Actions – (Options 1 & 2) - As the group goes with the tidal flow, perform the necessary capsize recoveries. As the paddlers get back into their boats and ready themselves to paddle, one of the unoccupied kayakers should be using that time to find an appropriate campsite since night is approaching. Knowing two of the group had already capsized in these conditions, getting off of the water should be a high priority. If possible, find a destination direction that has less tidal and wind resistance.

Summary – Even though the group misjudged the conditions, they knew there were currents and wind. In addition, when crossing open water to an island, there is a better than average chance winds can be funneling through that space. It is near sunset, which means the group did not leave a margin for error in case something went wrong, which it did. Higher fatigue levels at the end of the day should be taken into consideration before making crossings in rough conditions. The better decision would have been to make the crossing in the morning when the paddlers would be rested.

Dealing with capsizes has to be the top priority because of exposure concerns. Once everyone is ready to continue, getting off the water is essential, as mentioned above. After a capsize, self-confidence is usually lower with an increase in anxiety, which leads to stiffer torsos, which leads to higher chance of capsizing again since these two paddlers already went over in these conditions before the added stress of the first capsize. This is when solid land, warm clothes and a hot chocolate are called for.

Scenario #23 - Panicked Swimmer
One of your friends is panicking in the water after they did a wet exit. You paddle up next to them to try to calm them down. They freak out and grab you and try to climb onto your kayak. What is your course of action?

Event – Panicked swimmer climbing onto my kayak

Evaluate – They are panicking. I cannot remain upright with the extra person on my kayak.

116

Goals – Stay upright; get the person off of my kayak, try to calm the person and get them out of the water.

Options – 1) Push the swimmer away and get some distance from them. 2) Try to reason with the swimmer not to climb onto the kayak. 3) Let them climb on and try to stay upright with my sculling brace.

Actions – (Option 1) - I need to stay upright so I am in a better position to help the panicked swimmer. A person in panic does not usually respond well to reason. I decide to get away from them and try to reason with them while they are away from my kayak. If need be, I will paddle around to the other side of their kayak hoping they will grab onto their kayak instead of mine. Even if they don't, I will have their kayak to use as a stable platform if they decide to climb on mine. I am not concerned with drowning because the swimmer is wearing a PFD. I would not be paddling with someone who was not so equipped.

Summary – This is an example of a novice mistake. You never get near a person in the water until you can establish they are calm and can listen to and follow instructions. As you approach, a simple question to ask a swimmer who does not look calm is, "If you can hear me, tap your head with your right hand three times." If they do what I ask, it shows me they are able to listen, differentiate the correct hand to use and then perform the action. This shows they are listening and can follow instructions.

When I approach a paddler who is in the water, I keep their kayak between us. This way they cannot climb onto my kayak because there is a boat between us. As mentioned above, I can use their boat as a floating island of support if I need it.

As an instructor I have seen many students panic. I have learned that reason does not work quickly. Panic is an uncontrolled action. If the victim were able to remain calm, they would. They did not suddenly say, "I think I will panic now!" On one occasion, a slap to the helmet with a paddle was the only way to break the panic. My favorite method is to back paddle away from the panicked person so they expend some of that energy trying to catch me. In a short time they begin to calm down. As I back-paddle, I am speaking to them loudly. Eventually they respond and the dialog begins. Once I know they are clam, we can work out what to do.

I learned this the hard way when I volunteered to be a safety boater for a pier-to-pier swim in Santa Barbara, California. I was new to kayaking and learned that safety boaters were needed for this race. I figured it would be nice to paddle along the beautiful coast and watch the swimmers at the same time and assist if needed.

All of a sudden one of the swimmers stopped and looked around and then headed toward me. When he was close to my kayak he said he was very cold and he needed to get out of the water. The motorized support craft was nowhere to be seen. I saw the swimmer was shivering, so I decided he needed to lie over my back deck to get his trunk out of the water. I told him what to do and he said OK. However, when he climbed on, he tried to sit on my back deck as one does when riding on the back of a motorcycle.

I yelled out he needed to just lie on my back deck because this was too unstable. He wasn't listening. The kayak was shaking from side to side as I tried to stay upright with my bracing. In retrospect I figured the shaking kayak put him over the edge and he began to panic. He grabbed me with both of his arms. By doing so I could not use my paddle. I immediately reverted to my lifeguard training and flipped over with the hope he would let go and swim to the surface. I executed a super fast roll and when upright I paddled away as quickly as possible.

After getting a sufficient distance from the swimmer I turned around and moved slowly towards him. He frantically swam towards me. I started paddling backwards while shouting out to him. He eventually calmed down and we were able to come to an agreement as to how he needed to lie across my kayak.

I learned a lot that day. I share this story because most paddlers are not sufficiently trained to be rescue boaters. As a result of that experience, I developed skills just for this occasion. More importantly I learned how to avoid the panicked swimmer scenario. Think twice before you volunteer to be a safety boater. Swimmers do not wear life jackets. If you carry an extra floatation device, which can be tossed to a swimmer, you can avoid a lot of anguish.

Scenario #24 - Cold and Wet Paddler

On a sunny day, one of the members of your group of four paddlers capsizes and wet exits in the cold water. They are wearing boots, polypropylene long johns, shorts, a PFD and a short sleeve cotton shirt. They are having difficulty climbing back into their boat and they keep falling back into the water even though their kayak is being is stabilized. The paddler in the water is now showing visible signs of being too cold, due to the water temperature. What is your course of action?

Event – Paddler cannot re-enter their kayak and is showing signs of being to cold.

Evaluate – High priority because of exposure to cold water. Cannot climb onto their kayak unassisted.

Goals – Get the paddler back in their kayak and find ways to warm the paddler.

Options – 1) Try to drag the paddler up onto their kayak. 2) Have another paddler get in the water and push from below while another boater pulls from above. 3) Use a stirrup so the paddler can use their legs while they are being pulled up. 4) Do a scoop rescue, which is partially filling their kayak with water and let them slide into their cockpit. Once in the cockpit roll the kayak upright and pump out the water.

5) When they are back in their kayak they need to get into warm, dry clothing.

Actions – (Option 3 & 5) - Even though the paddler in the water is getting cold, the large muscles of the lower limbs should still be functional. They should be able to get up on their kayak if they are being pulled from above as they step up in the stirrup.

After they are in their cockpit, have them get out of the wet cotton shirt and dry them off as much as possible. If one is available, get them into a warm, dry shirt. Getting them to generate some body heat, by paddling, should be done as soon as they are ready to move. If there is enough radiant heat from the sun, use that as an external heat source. Putting a wind shell over their shirt will help keep heat in, if the sun's heat is not enough.

Summary – It is obvious this paddler is dressed incorrectly for the water temperature. The rule of thumb for kayakers is, *dress for the water temperature, not the air temperature.* There are many ways to cool down if you are wearing a wetsuit or a dry suit. Cold shock and hypothermia are both debilitating and can eventually lead to death. That is why paddlers should dress for immersion.

Loss of upper body strength happens quickly in cold water. That is why each paddler should carry a stirrup. Being able to step up onto your kayak is a lot easier than trying to climb on with just your arms. It is also invaluable if you have to get back into your boat if you could not use one of your arms due to an injury during a capsize, such as straining a shoulder, when trying to roll or brace.

If the stirrup didn't work I would try the scoop rescue next. These are one of those rarely used techniques that every kayaker needs to know. My last option would be putting another paddler in the water to help push the cold swimmer up into their kayak. If the paddler had dressed properly, then a regular assisted recovery would have done the trick and

120

this would not be a scenario. Even though the frequency of this mistake has dropped significantly, I still hear or read about them.

Scenario #25 - Flying Kayak

As you are driving down the highway you see through the rear view mirror a crash occur behind you because one of your kayaks flew off of the top of your van. You pull over and run back and see a multi-car accident with your kayak through the windshield of one of the cars. In addition, your passengers have started to follow you. What is your course of action?

Event – Car accident due to your kayak. Your passengers are running along the side of the highway.

Evaluate – Accident that needs evaluating. Concern for the safety of my passengers.

Goals – Help if there are injuries; keep my passengers from becoming victims; get emergency vehicles on scene and try to prevent additional car accidents.

Options – 1) Have your passengers try to slow and manage traffic without becoming victims. 2) Evaluate the result of your kayak going through the windshield. 3) Call 911 for the accident, as you run over to the damaged car and keep them on the line as you determine if medical assistance is needed.

Actions – I would do all three options. I would provide whatever medical assistance I could if there were injuries. I would be very concerned about the first few cars coming on the scene because they could cause another accident if they were not paying attention. Once the traffic was slowed and being managed, then another accident would be less likely. Getting professional emergency assistance is a must.

Summary – Whether you caused the accident or not, being able to provide assistance in the form of first aid or traffic control should be in your skills set. Because you will be driving to and from your adventures, carrying flares and flashlights are a good idea, along with a high visibility vest in case of road accidents or stalled vehicles.

The primary reason for this scenario is the necessity to secure your kayaks properly to your roof racks. I see too many drivers who neglect to use bow and stern tie-offs. They think the rack will do the job. Unfortunately, racks do come off of roofs and/or break due to stress. I have had the rack attachment snap on two different occasions due to strong side winds blowing on the kayak. The torque produced is significant. The bow and stern tie-downs will not keep the rack from breaking, but they will keep the boats from flying off of your car. How would you feel if one of your loved ones was impaled and killed by a kayak coming through their windshield? It is your responsibility to keep your boats on your car. They can become lethal projectiles if not secured properly.

A note of caution regarding bow and stern tie-offs, don't forget to secure them before you drive away. I know of a couple that backed over the lines and the pull on the ropes caused their kayaks to crack. Tie off the lines and remember to use red flags if the boats are 3 or more feet beyond the rear bumper.

If you like reviewing paddle related incidents, I highly recommend you read *Deep Trouble* and *More Deep Trouble*, which are a collection of kayaker mistakes, edited by Sea Kayaker Magazine. The authors, George Gronseth and Matt Broze, review the incidents so we can learn from the mistakes of others.

CHAPTER 7

RISK ASSESSMENT
Risk-Adventure-Safe

Of the twenty-four lens-factors listed in the decision-making lens chapter, risk assessment was one I felt needed to be addressed in more depth. Mother Nature can present us with numerous challenges, with some of them being life threatening. Being able to assess (identify and evaluate) those possible threats is a lens-factor you are going to be using regularly, so you should have a clear understanding of yours, because recognizing and avoiding dangerous situations is infinitely better to being caught in them.

Since "Adventurer" is included in the title of this book I feel it is important to briefly explore the relationship between adventure, risk and safe. Let's begin by defining all three:
- Adventure is an undertaking usually involving danger and risks.
- Risk is the possibility of loss or injury and/or exposure to hazard or danger.
- Safe is free from harm.

During the first few years of directing UCSB's Adventure Programs I saw an interesting contradiction with respect to our clientele. They desired adventure, but they also wanted assurances that they would be safe. Since adventure, by definition, has to include some element of risk or danger, it cannot be considered safe.

Knowing this, I eliminated the word "safe" from all of our literature because I knew I could not guarantee to any client they would be "free from harm" during any of our offerings. My personal belief is, "safe does not exist." Two days before writing this sentence a news story reported that a plane had crashed into a house, killing the occupants inside as they were preparing to watch the Super Bowl game. I am willing to bet they thought they were safe in their home. We are always surrounded by some element of risk.

Instead of "safe," I began using "acceptable level of risk" in our advertising literature regarding our trips and classes. I wanted to set the expectation that risk was involved. I also wanted our clients to start thinking about assessing risk and hoping they would ask, "What do you mean by acceptable?" Believe it or not, not once during my 25-year tenure, did I hear that question. If they only had known that the person saying it was "acceptable" also loves kayaking over waterfalls.

Even though I eliminated the word "safe," I do use the word "safety" when it is appropriate. I think it is important to note the difference between the two words and how they are used because it can get a bit confusing. Here are some examples:
- We use the latest safety devices.
- We have established safety procedures.
- While your safety is our concern, we cannot guarantee you will be safe.
- We do guarantee your safety, is an example of safety=safe.

At one time I read some literature from Outward Bound warning their instructors to be on the lookout for certain "risk traits" within their participants. They were:
- "*Immortals*" - Those who showed no fear for any activity;
- "*Abdicators*" - Ones who believed others would make sure they were safe;
- "*Disembodied*" - Those who don't pay attention and walk right into danger.

These traits, when exhibited by participants, should be a red flag to any trip leader with respect to risk assessment. I believe it is the responsibility of all guides to discuss identifying, assessing and managing risks with their groups before embarking on any adventure.

Since risk is often a personal perception, it is up to the individual to decide what is an acceptable level. I use the steps of the DMP for my personal risk assessment and that of the group when I am leading.

- *Event* - Able to identify the risk.
- *Evaluate* - Rate the risk level (real vs. perceived); Can I handle it?
- *Goals* - Ultimately to stay alive for another adventure.
- *Options* - Finding ways to do it, or avoid it.
- *Action* - Do it or don't do it.
- *Results* - If you are successful, you've chosen wisely; if not, *"ouch"* or worse.

As I suggested earlier, an acceptable level of risk is relative to the perception of the person viewing it. Your skills, experience and your self-confidence will be huge factors in your decision to take on or avoid the challenge. Ego and reputation should NOT be factors when you decide.

My good friend Dick Rice, professional outdoor guide and instructor, sent me this little risk questionnaire when I told him I was writing this book. He uses it in his courses. It is his way of conducting a brief self-assessment regarding one's thoughts on risk. He adjusted it from one he received from the University of Oregon Outdoor Program. I too made some adjustments. The purpose of this questionnaire is to get you thinking about risk.

Risk Questionnaire:

Do you believe in challenge by choice? Why or why not?
   Strongly disagree 1-2-3-4-5-6-7-8-9-10 strongly agree

Risk is fun.
   Strongly disagree 1-2-3-4-5-6-7-8-9-10 strongly agree

You receive a higher level of satisfaction after completing a higher risk activity.
   Strongly disagree 1-2-3-4-5-6-7-8-9-10 strongly agree

Do you find you value the safety of others more than your own?
   Strongly disagree 1-2-3-4-5-6-7-8-9-10 strongly agree

You see a real difference between perceived risk and real risk.
   Strongly disagree 1-2-3-4-5-6-7-8-9-10 strongly agree

You find subjective risk factors to be more influential than objective factors.
   Strongly disagree 1-2-3-4-5-6-7-8-9-10 strongly agree

You actually practice risk management in your personal outdoor activities.
   Strongly disagree 1-2-3-4-5-6-7-8-9-10 strongly agree

There are adventure activities I would pursue personally, but not in a professional setting with a group.
   Strongly disagree 1-2-3-4-5-6-7-8-9-10 strongly agree

Before I started using the DMP steps regarding risk, I used the following questions to help me decide what to do:
- What are the possible dangers?
- How serious are the consequences?
- Can I handle the dangers as I see them?
- Am I willing to take the chance?
- How will my decision affect others?

The questionnaire and the questions above are just two ways to help you think about your own views regarding risk. As I said, I do not believe "safe" exists, so assessing potential risk should be a daily exercise. Aside from assessing it, I also feel one should address how they value risk.

I once read a letter Paul Petzoldt, founder of National Outdoor Leadership Schools (NOLS), wrote in reply to a mother's letter wanting some assurances that her son would be safe on his month long NOLS adventure. Here is a summary of his answer, as I recall it.

*Madam, I appreciate the concern you have for the welfare of
your son and desire he'd be safe. In fact, it is your job to watch
out for his well-being. Unfortunately I cannot guarantee his
safety. In fact, there exists a chance, although remote, he can
get injured or even killed during his trip. However, I can assure
you that if you are successful in your job of keeping him safe,
you will kill his soul.*

I recall getting quite emotional when I read Paul's letter for
the first time - and many times after. It struck a chord within
me about the value of taking risks. I know my life feels much
richer by the risks I have taken regardless if they were
successful or not. I have to admit adventure is a high priority
for me. The degree of adventure varies with the degree of
potential risk.

Regardless of the level, I am always aware that there is risk
every time I get into my kayak, ski in the backcountry, climb
a rock face or even swim in the ocean. This awareness keeps
me alert and gives me a greater sense of being alive. It is so
easy to lose one's sense of self in our daily routines. Even
though I have established routines for getting ready, no
matter how many times I get into my kayak, it is never
routine. One of the lures for me in sea kayaking is the
adventure. If there were no risks, there would be no
adventure.

An important point to keep in mind is, just because there is
potential danger it doesn't automatically mean you will get
hurt. It is the potential of loss or injury that eliminates safe
as a guaranteed commodity. It is amazing how awareness
changes when there is threat of risk or danger. For me, it
heightens my senses. Even though risk is a lure, I doubt
many would undertake an activity if there was 100%
certainty they would get injured while doing it.

Knowing the risks involved is critical in making an effective
decision. It is up to you to decide if the potential risk is worth
the adventure. My values on this subject are not meant to
push you into dangerous situations. My goal is for you to

consider the possible values of taking that chance during your assessment. Will it be safe? For me, I hope not!

"If the highest aim of a captain were to preserve his ship, he would keep it in port forever." - Thomas Aquinas

CHAPTER 8

WHAT TO KNOW BEFORE YOU GO

The purpose of this book is to examine the DMP, identify the factors that influence our decisions and then practice using that process through scenario reviews. Due to reoccurring tragedies I felt I would be remiss if I did not include this chapter since one of the major themes of this book is being proactive, which means avoiding dangerous situations whenever possible.

I formerly believed outdoor enthusiasts knew how to deal with the challenges Mother Nature would throw at them. If that were truly the case, why do I still see on the evening news, stories about the experienced hiker or the seasoned paddler being found dead in the elements? With that in mind let's look at the common reasons why adventurer's get into trouble in the outdoors. The information in this chapter should be included in your breadth of knowledge. Even if you think you know all there is about wilderness survival you may still find a useful nugget below.

Being outdoors is the common element of all adventures, which means we are dealing with a very dynamic environment. The other commonality is we are warm-blooded human beings and our bodies need to function properly in order to survive. Exposure to the elements is the most frequent reason for cause of death in the outdoors. Because temperatures are so variable; and food and water can be scarce, our decisions, training and proper planning should focus heavily on minimizing and/or avoiding exposure by understanding the many aspects of it.

It is important to note that our body and mind work best when normal body temperature is maintained, we are well hydrated and our nutritional intake supplies our body's needs. Upset any of the above requirements and our body stops functioning normally and eventually you will die. Our primary goal in any outdoor setting is to avoid, or at least minimize, upsetting our body's needs and normal function. Therefore, your decision-making lens and actions should consider these needs as high priority.

Having a thorough knowledge of first aid in wilderness settings may not only save a life, it might also relieve you of endless guilt after not being able to help someone else. I highly recommend a Wilderness First Aid Responder class. Since this is not a first aid book I am focusing on prevention and recognition, not treatment. I urge you to take a class to learn how to treat these conditions as well as many other illnesses and injuries. In addition, you should seriously consider attending an outdoor self-reliance/survival course, especially if you prefer solo adventures.

Exposure

Exposure includes, hypothermia (heat loss), hyperthermia (overheating) and dehydration (lack of water). Even though it is not truly exposure, one should also understand nutritional depravation (electrolyte imbalance and starvation).

Hypothermia

Hypothermia is when your core body temperature lowers to dangerous levels. The average normal body temperature is about 98.6°F/37°C. The most accurate way to measure core temperature is with a rectal thermometer. Rather than focus on your exact temperature you should be aware of both the early and late stage symptoms of hypothermia.

Early symptoms include:
- Shivering;
- Cold, pale, or blue-grey skin;
- Lack of interest or concern (apathy);
- Poor judgment;
- Mild unsteadiness in balance or walking;
- Slurred speech;
- Numb hands and fingers and problems performing tasks.

Late symptoms include:
- The trunk of the body is cold to the touch;
- Muscles becoming stiff;
- Slow pulse;
- Breathing that is shallow and slower;
- Weakness or sleepiness (lethargy);
- Confusion;
- Loss of consciousness;
- Shivering, which may stop if body temperature drops below 90°F/32°C.

While you may see these symptoms in others it is difficult to self-assess when you are hypothermic because your "self-evaluation" is impaired (Stumble, Mumble, Fumble and Jumble). The key is not to get hypothermic.

Heat loss
Knowing how your body loses heat gives you the basis on how to prevent/minimize that loss. Here are the ways in which we lose body heat so you can deal with it accordingly.

Conduction
Direct contact with a cold objects or liquids, such as sleeping on cold ground without insulation, causes the heat to transfer towards the colder object. Therefore keep insulating layers between you and cold objects. Stand on a closed cell foam pad when snow camping to keep your feet warmer. Wear a wetsuit or a dry suit when in cool/cold water. Wear multiple layers and avoid cotton when outside in cold weather.

Radiation
The heat from your body radiates out through the skin as heat radiates from a wood stove. Wearing clothes keeps the heat from radiating too far away from the body. Some garments have an aluminum foil type layer sewn in to reflect radiant heat back toward your body. The type and amount of layering can reduce heat loss and even hold that radiant heat near your body.

Evaporation

When your sweat evaporates it cools your skin. You don't want to stop sweating, but you do not want to sweat too much. That is why it is important to wear multiple layers. You can add or subtract layers to get the right combination to keep you warm. Overheating increases sweat production. You want to wear clothing that wicks the moisture away from your body (fleece and wool) because your body will try to warm the wet clothing, especially cotton, thus losing more heat. Wearing a wet cotton t-shirt on a hot day is good to cool you down, but not when it is cold and you are trying to maintain body heat.

Convection

Loss of heat due to wind or water flowing past your skin is convection. Your body heats the air and water (if in the water) that is right next to the skin. If the wind blows that heated air away from your skin or you move your body through the air, your body has to heat more air. The same thing happens when you are in the water. Wearing a wind shell or other layering will eliminate convection heat loss in air; as will a wetsuit or dry suit in the water.

Respiration

If you inhale cold air, your body has to heat it. When you exhale, there is heat loss with each breath. However, you cannot stop breathing, but you can wear a facemask in extreme cold conditions, which will help reduce this loss.

Clothing and Layering

Unless you have a garment that actually has a heating element in it (like an electric blanket) your clothing does not technically "warm" you in colder conditions. You may feel warm, but your clothing is only slowing your heat loss. This is an important point because eventually you will get hypothermic if you cannot maintain your body heat through insulation and fueling it. On the flip side, if you cannot cool your body properly in hot conditions, you could overheat.

In cold air your goal with respect to layering is to address the reasons your body loses heat. A thin wicking layer next to the body will deal with convection and some evaporation. At the same time your body is heating the material of the thin layer (conduction) from the inside and the colder air is cooling the fabric from the outside, which cause more heat loss. The more layers you have the less heat your body will lose because the cold does not cool the multiple layers as quickly. In layering you are trying to create dead air spaces, which slows down the cold influence. Multiple layers, with the last one being a rain/wind shell, work the best.

When immersed in water, a proper fitting wetsuit allows a thin layer of water to fill the spaces between your skin and the closed cell material of the suit. Your body then heats this thin layer and you will actually feel warm after the initial chill of the water entering the suit. If that thin layer of water is not being replaced then heat loss due to convection is not an issue, nor is there heat loss from evaporation either. However, if it is a loose fitting wet suit, then convection becomes an issue. Once your body has heated that water between you and the suit it now tries to heat the suit as well. The cold water is now acting to cool the suit (conduction in action). The thicker the suit, the longer before you feel chilled. Despite wearing a wetsuit in cold water, you will eventually become cold.

A dry suit is a thin fabric that does not insulate very well, but is designed to keep the water outside and not in direct contact with your body. You lose a lot more heat when your body tries to heat water compared to air - up to 25 times faster in water than in air. The success of a dry suit is in the layers you wear under the suit. I wear multiple thick layers when I know I will be standing in the water for a few hours working with my students. If I wore those same layers on a tour I would overheat. Your goal is to layer inside your dry suit to both prevent overheating and to insulate you for immersion.

I have regularly told my students there is no such thing as bad weather, just inappropriate clothing. I wrote an article for my website (www.useakayak.org - Reflections from the Cockpit link) called "The Dressing Game" because I consider how you dress for the anticipated conditions a competition; your comfort vs. the environment. Even though it focuses on dressing for kayaking, the concepts in the article are relevant for any outdoor activity. If you dress properly for the conditions you win; if not, you lose, and your final score can be life threatening or even deadly.

Along with proper layering, learning how to build effective shelters can keep you dry, while maintaining some heat and keeping you out of the wind, which is equally imperative.

Hyperthermia
Perspiration is your body's cooling mechanism. On a hot day you can use the factors of heat loss to help you maintain your body's normal temperature. If your core temperature reaches or exceeds 104°F/40°C your life could be at risk. Of the two main overheating illnesses, Heat Stroke is the more serious because it can be life threatening. It requires immediate action.

Heat exhaustion symptoms include:
- Cool moist skin with goose bumps when in the heat;
- Heavy sweating;
- Faintness;
- Dizziness;
- Weak, rapid pulse;
- Low blood pressure upon standing;
- Muscle cramps.

Heat stroke symptoms include:
- Headache;
- A very high fever 104°F/40°C;
- Disorientation;
- Confusion;
- Bright red flushed looking skin;
- Sweating possibly stops.

Too high and too much external heat can cause your body to overheat. Your goals are to cool your body and/or reduce the hotter conditions. The evaporation from perspiration is your body's main cooling mechanism. You want to let it do that by not covering up your skin. Having air move past your body also helps your cooling mechanism. Since you lose more heat in water than in air, getting into water will be helpful. Wetting and wearing a cotton hat can help cool you since you can lose significant heat through your head.

Before the increase in awareness of the harmful rays of the sun, many didn't cover their bodies, which helped our cooling mechanism. Now minimizing the amount of skin exposed to the sun can adversely affect your cooling by evaporation. If you wear lightweight protective clothing and keep it wet you are substituting conduction for evaporation as the cooling mechanism. How often you wet your clothing and the temperature of the water will be your guide.

Even though exposing yourself to direct sunlight is not immediately life threatening, there are some things worth mentioning. Wearing adequate sunglasses is important for the long and short-term health of your eyes. However, when sunlight (specifically UV rays) reflects off of snowfields, bright landscapes and even water, these extreme light conditions can damage your eyes within a few hours. It is sunburn of your eyes. This is important because your eyesight is critical for getting around. You can also get severe sunburn to exposed skin, which is very painful and it can also affect your mobility due to swelling. The long-term affects of sun exposure have proven to be fatal due to skin cancer.

During one of my Hawaii kayaking trips, one of the participants neglected to put sunscreen on the top of his feet. Even though he was an expert paddler, with decades of experience, he had never paddled a sit-on-top kayak in such sunlit conditions. The following day his previous lily-white feet, now beet red, ballooned up and he couldn't walk for two days due to intense pain.

Dehydration

We need water to live. If we do not get water our body shuts down different systems until we die. Before we die, that lack of water adversely affects our electrolyte balance, which could be one of the contributing factors of heat exhaustion and heat stroke. Your goal is to stay well hydrated. Your urine is an excellent indicator if you are getting enough water. It should be clear/light yellow and copious (plentiful). Infrequent nature calls with very yellow urine means you are not getting enough water. Constipation can also be an indicator.

Perspiration, respiration, urination and defecation are the main ways we lose water. Unfortunately we cannot, nor do we want to, stop these processes so we need to remain hydrated. That being the case, you should find a system that allows you to drink regularly.

Before the advent of bladders with tubes I used water bottles. Many times it was a hassle to get to the bottles, often stopping my forward progress when hiking or paddling so I didn't drink as often as I should have. Now that I have a water system that places a tube right near my mouth, from my pack or my PFD, I am regularly drinking water. I know this as a fact because I am refilling the bladder more often.

You can only carry so much water, especially if you are hiking. Therefore having a water purification system needs to be a priority in your equipment list aside from identifying enough water sources on your planned route.

Nutrition

Regularly fueling your body is essential. How you do it is up to you. The only advice I am going to give you is to carry extra food on any adventure. Powdered energy drinks will help you maintain your electrolytes in an emergency. Add a couple of power bars and you have some emergency rations that won't take up much space with minimal weight.

When Stuck or Lost
Those doing overnight adventures are prepared and equipped for the extended stay. Unfortunately, the vast majority of outdoor tragedies have been day-trippers who have become unplanned overnighters. It is most often the day hiker who gets lost or sprains an ankle too far from trailhead. It may be the mountain biker whose bike falls apart at the farthest point of the ride. Perhaps a cross-country skier gets caught in a sudden whiteout and cannot get out before dark. Since in none of these scenarios was there a plan to be out for the night, here are a few tips you may find useful to consider before heading out for that day excursion.

Mental state - Maintaining a **P**ositive **M**ental **A**ttitude (PMA) in an emergency is essential. If you panic your DMP will suffer. Staying positive allows you to make an accurate assessment of your situation. It is best to work through one problem at a time so you do not get overwhelmed.

Lost - Being lost means you do not know where you are and more importantly, you do not know in which direction to travel to get to out. The consistent advice I have heard from Search & Rescue personnel is to stay in one place when you are lost. If you keep wandering you may be missing the very people who are looking for you. Find a place with good shelter and water if possible. Then try signaling from that location. Paying attention to your progress, with respect to the terrain and landmarks, and knowing how to use a topo' map and a compass are your best defenses against getting lost. Of course you left your itinerary/float plan with a responsible individual before you took off on your trip.

Signaling - There are different methods for signaling, including sound, visual and electronic devices.

Sound is good for short distance. Whistles, banging, shouting or any other regular sounds could help someone find your location if they are within earshot. I like the whistle best because it can be used regularly when you exhale. It is lightweight, small and can also be used to scare wildlife away from your location. Avoid shouting unless you hear someone calling you. Your voice will give out quickly if used too much.

Visual signals can be seen at a greater distance compared to the range of sound. Fires, smoke, flashlights, mirrors, flares, reflective tape, water dyes and a large SOS written out in the open can attract someone's attention. If you are out in the forest, using any type of fire or incendiary device can cause a forest fire that can end up killing you and many more, so use such methods carefully.

Electronic devices include cell phones, radios, and satellite phones and locators. They are dependent on battery life so extra batteries should be considered. Cell phones are dependent on service towers. Radios are dependent on the range and the terrain. Satellite phones and locators work almost everywhere, but are usually the most expensive. Do your research and decide what will work best for you.

I have a friend who says having a fishing hook with some line is your best way to get found. Drop that line in the nearest creek, river or lake and make sure you do not have a fishing license. He swears a ranger will be there in an instant. I am not sure I would count on this to get rescued, but you may end up with a nice meal.

Necessary Equipment

The comedian George Carlin has joked that you can't have everything, because where would you put it? Everyone who writes about survival will have their own list of necessary items. If you are out on an overnight trip you will probably have lots of equipment with you. My concern is focused more for the day-tripper who inadvertently needs to spend at least one unplanned night outside. Weight and space are important consideration for a day outing. Knowing it is possible to get caught outside overnight I keep these items in

138

my daypack (day bag when kayaking) at all times for the following reasons: (See *Appendix 1* for the full list)

Knife – My "go to" preference is my Swiss Army knife that has a host of tools aside from the two cutting blades (saw, corkscrew, awl, scissors, can opener, screwdriver, bottle opener, tweezers and a toothpick). There are numerous tools like this on the market that have the combination of blades/items you prefer. Some prefer larger fixed blade knives, which have advantages for chopping, but weigh more. The important point is having a cutting blade. The other bells and whistles can be extremely helpful and choosing which ones will be a matter of your priorities.

A good knife is a foundational tool, which can help you make other tools, such as spears for hunting and fishing. It is the primary tool for shelter building, repairs, carving, notching and even fire making (kindling, sparker, etc...). It is a very critical piece of gear.

Fire starter – Even though one can start a fire through friction and wood, if available (a la Tom Hanks in *Castaway*), I carry a couple of different means of starting a fire without having to do too much work. I have waterproof matches and some match/fire starter mini blocks. Both are kept in a mini zip-lock bag. There are many different methods (matches, spark kits, flint/steel friction starters, lighters, etc...) sold in hunting/sporting goods stores for getting your warming fire going. Having an immediate heat source (matches or lighter) lets you sterilize a blade quickly, instead of having to wait for a fire. Aside from providing warmth, fires are used for signaling, sterilizing water, light, protection, cooking and psychological comfort. In addition, how can you possibly tell a scary story without a campfire?

Headlamp *(LED) w/extra batteries* – Being able to see at night is mandatory for me. I prefer a headlamp because it allows hands-free operation. Mine is waterproof with two light levels (high and low beams), plus a strobe and red light feature. It also has a second strap that goes over my head to keep the light from slipping down without having to make the main strap so tight that it gives me a headache. The LED light with extra batteries gives me longer light time. Aside from providing light, it is also a signaling device.

Whistle – I find a whistle is the most compact signaling device available for short distance alerts. I prefer a plastic whistle without that little ball inside (which can inhibit function if it freezes or gets stuck). It can also be good for frightening (hopefully) wildlife away from your location. Your voice will give out in a short time, but you can blow a whistle as long as you are breathing.

Topo' maps/charts – Reading my topo' map as I hike not only keeps me on my chosen path, it shows me my relative location to my destination point and allows me to calculate my pace. It also shows me other options if I need/want to go off trail. Maps can also help you identify water sources, clearings and high points for viewing and signaling. The only times I do not take maps are on short, well-traveled, well-maintained trail hikes.

When I kayak, my charts are on the front deck of my kayak, in a waterproof pouch, so I can identify the water and shore features along the way. I also carry topo' maps, which provide more details of the land features compared to the information on nautical charts. The chart/map paper can also be used to help start a fire if absolutely needed.

Compass w/mirror & magnifying lens – My handheld compass has many features aside from the magnetic needle. It has a mirror to be used for signaling, aside from getting more precise readings; a magnifying lens for seeing small features and for possibly starting a fire from concentrating sunlight; and a slope meter for assessing avalanche potential. I have rarely used my compass on land because I follow my progress on the topo' map, but I know how to use it to find my location, with respect to the map.

140

I regularly use my deck-mounted compass when kayaking to help me stay on course, especially on open waterways. If one doesn't have a compass in fog you will literally paddle in circles because everyone is stronger on one side than the other and without a reference point you cannot even tell you are circling. A deck-mounted compass also reduces the chance of getting seasick because you are still looking out towards the horizon when viewing the compass compared to using a handheld one on your spray skirt, which forces you to look down too often. I do carry my handheld one in my day bag for the other uses mentioned.

Cordage *(nylon about 50-100 ft)* – Nylon cord (commonly referred to as parachute cord) has infinite uses. Here are a few from my years of adventures:
- Slings;
- Splints;
- Shelters;
- Repairs;
- Hanging food;
- Snares;
- Clothesline (drying clothes over fire);
- Tie downs;
- Avalanche cord.

Space blanket – Using this little, well-packed, blanket of reflective material is a great way to stay dry, block the wind and rain while reducing the loss of your body heat. It can be used to gather water, create a shelter and secure a splint, just to mention a few other uses. It is a great emergency tool, aside from being very affordable.

Plastic bag (large leaf size - 44 gallon) – I have seen these bags used as:
- Rain ponchos;
- Water carriers;
- Paddle jackets;
- Wind shells;
- Shelter material;
- Sleeping bags;

- Splint wrapping;
- Water gathering devices;
- Carrying trash you pick up on your way out.

I am confident I can survive a few nights in the outdoors with these few items. I may get hungry but I will be able to minimize exposure issues, which is my greatest concern. I want to thank Lee Moyer, kayak designer and engineer, for sharing his sage advice about only taking equipment along that has at least three uses. It has taught me to think about the potential versatility of all my equipment.

When I go on a day hike I normally have my watch, a water system, hiking poles, some food, cell-phone w/battery back-up and I am dressed for the forecasted conditions, with one additional outside upper layer of clothing, usually a wind/rain shell. A cap and gloves are also standard in my daypack. Again, check *Appendix 1* for my different equipment lists.

CHAPTER 9

LEADERS - PARTICIPANTS - GROUPS
DMP Considerations

The DMP I have been explaining, up to this point, has been mostly focusing on the decisions you make for yourself. There are added considerations that *Leaders*, *Participants* and *Groups* should take into account when making decisions. These considerations are not really lens-factors, so I call them elemental concerns.

Leaders

I will be using the terms **Leader or Guide** interchangeably to refer to anyone who is responsible for making decisions that affect those in their charge. I will use **Professional**, if the person in charge is being paid for their service. Whether you are paid to lead or you volunteer, you have tremendous responsibilities with respect to managing the well-being of others. I have included a number of elemental concerns that leaders will find useful when working with groups.

Expectations of A Leader

During the first night's lecture in my Leadership Training Course, I have the group call out what they expect from an outdoor leader as I list the responses on the board. The list tends to get quite long. Here are just a few of the frequently expressed expectations:

- Responsible for group safety;
- Adequate *First Aid* and emergency training;
- Ability to handle emergencies, while remaining calm and confident;
- Know their job and the environment;
- Good people skills (diverse personalities and populations);
- Good communicator (clear and audible)
- Experienced in group dynamics;
- Provide a good time;
- Being prepared and punctual;
- Staying alert;

- Knows all the answers.

One year there were almost 100 expectations written on the board. Often times there were items that were polarized; such as: stick to the advertised itinerary vs. make it up as we go along; be punctual vs. don't be the time police; tell us about every rock and tree vs. let us enjoy the quiet and tranquility of the outdoors. My personal favorite is, I want a real adventure, but I want it to be safe.

Whether you think these expectations are warranted or not, makes no difference. If you are viewed as the "leader," then your **thinking of others** lens-factor needs to be one of priority. If you are a *Professional*, these expectations virtually become demands, because clients feel entitled when they pay for an adventure. I once heard a fellow guide refer to these expectations as an *Unspoken Burden*. While I understand the sentiment, if you feel these expectations are a burden, you should reconsider your choice of being a guide.

As a leader, you do have tremendous responsibilities. The key is to know the difference between your true responsibilities and the unrealistic expectations you feel you are carrying. Remember, just because a group member has an expectation does not mean it is your responsibility to fulfill it. My suggestion to all leaders is to make a list of your true responsibilities and make it part of your personal *Mission Statement* for leading. This way, when a decision needs to be made you can refer to that statement as part of your DMP.

I raise this point because I have seen too many instances where leaders have made unwise decisions by trying to cater to some of the group's unrealistic and/or risky expectations, believing it was their responsibility to do so.

Another good thing about being clear about your responsibilities, and what you will be providing as a leader, is it can help you to set realistic expectations when

144

advertising your trip. Not only does this take the self-imposed pressure off of you, it can help minimize possible disappointment of those in the group.

Assessing Your Group

Making decisions that affect your entire group or individual members might be easier if you know more about each member. It would be great if you could perform *Spock's Vulcan mind-meld technique* on each participant at the beginning of the trip. This way you would know their expectations, likes, dislikes, strengths, weaknesses, health issues and, most importantly, their major concerns. As an example, if you knew each individual's risk trait (immortal, abdicator or disembodied) at the start of the trip, you would have more information for your DMP. Assuming you are not a Vulcan, you need to begin your assessment as soon as you can. Here are ways to do just that:

- Trip questionnaire and/or checklist;
- Planned questions for your group introduction circle;
- Listening to and watching each member;

While I philosophically believe all participants should be treated the same and/or equally, my experience has shown me everyone is different. That being the case, I adjust my methods so I can get the best out of each member. What I endeavor to do is treat everyone fairly. One of my foundation principles, with respect to managing individuals, is "You gotta know your people."

What I try to assess about individuals, and the group as a whole:

- Medical histories (including dietary restrictions);
- Medications needed, how to administer and their location;
- Experience (specific to the trip, and in general);
- Strengths (physically and capabilities);
- Weaknesses (physically and capabilities);
- Awareness;
- Endurance;
- Skills;

- Communication style;
- Interaction with others;
- Their projection (body language, facial expressions, eye contact, posture and respiration rhythm)
- Expectations;
- Desires;
- Passions;
- Concerns;
- Group pace;
- Group norms;
- Group cooperation;
- Group interactions.

I would be lying if I told you I assess all of this on every trip, for each individual. I can say, I do my best within the time I have with the group. Once I learned how to tune into these different elements, it enhanced my DMP and actions. As I mentioned in the lens chapter, "The richer your lens, the more effective the decision."

Leader's Expectations of the Group

Participants are not the only ones who may have unrealistic expectations. I know I was guilty of this early in my career. In fact, I recall lamenting to a close friend, "I wonder why there are not many seasoned backpackers signing up for our trips?" My buddy replied with this question, "Would you sign up for one of your trips?" My immediate reply was, No! My answer to his next obvious question was, "I prefer going by myself or with a few friends, instead of having to deal with a group."

This made me think about what type of individuals would sign up for my trip and why? Not only would it help me in what they would expect, it could also let me know what I could expect. Here is another insight I had as a result of one of my staff interviewing me for their Environmental Studies class.

I was asked to define my concept of wilderness. After a couple of minutes of thought, I said, "any place where you feel

*threatened by your environment, due to not knowing it." My
answer did not include anything about being out in the woods
or in remote areas. I told my staff member, "I feel more
comfortable in the mountains, compared to some of the tough
neighborhoods in New York City, where I grew up, because
bears don't carry guns." I was trying to relay the concept that
wilderness is more a state of mind, than a location.*

I then shared a little bit of my Outward Bound experience to
bring home my point.

*On the third night of my month-long mountaineering course in
the Three Sisters Wilderness in Oregon, I was asked to escort
our two patrol leaders back to their sleeping area because
they left their flashlights in camp. On my return trip, by myself,
I imagined all kinds of monsters lurking just outside of my
lighted path, ready to attack me. I specifically had visions of
the Creature from the Black Lagoon with his huge, clawed,
webbed hands reaching out and grabbing me by the throat. I
began to sprint the 100 yards back to camp. When I saw my
group in the firelight, I let out a hushed sigh of relief. I strolled
into camp looking calm and collected - with my heart racing
at 100 miles per hour.*

*Three weeks later, I recall getting up in the middle of the night
for a nature call. I slipped on my boots, which is all I had on.
After returning to my sleeping bag, I realized I had just been
squatting for a minute or two and walking naked in the
"Wilderness" without a flashlight, and I was as calm as could
be. The monsters were gone!*

My environment was no longer "Wilderness" to me. I learned
about my surroundings and I was extremely comfortable.
Which leads me to my point; people who sign-up for guided
trips oftentimes feel they are entering the vast unknown
wilderness. The fear of the unknown is one most of us share.
If we do not know it, we are cautious. This is something you
should expect from your participants.

Not thinking is another phenomenon I have often seen while guiding. It is common for clients to wait to be told regarding actions they would normally do on their own. I have to hold my NY cynicism when asked:

- Should I put on my coat?
- Can I eat now?
- Where can I sit?
- Should I stay in the tent or sleep out?

These people are not stupid, but they seem to turn off their brain rather than taking the time to really think about what they are asking. What I find dangerous is - what does this "non-thinking" mean to their risk awareness and management? I believe the majority of participants on organized trips with designated leaders (especially professional ones), become abdicators with respect to their personal safety. Be prepared and try to be proactive in getting them to keep their brains working.

Leader's Decision-Making Style
Every leader has their particular style, with respect to leadership and decision-making. I am going to focus on decision-making styles, because leadership methodology is not within the scope of this book. I have seen three dominant methods of deciding, among the thousand plus leaders I have observed, over the years. They are:

- Decide - act;
- Decide - rethink - act;
- Keep thinking - decide - act.

I will not tell you what I think is the best style. I feel there are pros and cons for each, which I will share with you. Some leaders may have a preferred style, while others may switch depending on the situation.

Decide - Act
If you have to decide and act immediately, this style is great. If you have time before you need to act, then not thinking about your decision means your mind is clear to deal with other things. In this instance, you have made your decision

and then moved on to your next priority. However, if there is any time lag between your decision and initiating action, taking time to reconsider could be prudent, in case of changes in the event.

Decide - Rethink - Act
If you need to act immediately, this style may cause hesitation. If there is a time delay for action, this style may give you the best results if changes occur in the event. However, as mentioned above, this rethinking may keep your mind from focusing on other things.

Keep Thinking - Decide - Act
This style is not conducive to events that need immediate attention. If you are one who takes too much time to decide, your hesitation may produce negative results, because you missed your time to act. Waiting until the last minute does have possible advantages, with respect to considering more factors, if time allows.

Personally, depending on the situation, I use all three. My default method is a combination of the first two. I can decide and act immediately if needed. If there is a time delay, I will decide and rethink just before the time to act, in case of new information. I do not spend the entire lag time rethinking my decision. I caution all leaders not to get stuck on just one style, because it will not work in all situations.

There is one more thing I need to add to this discussion with respect to your decision making style. Are you a leader who feels they need to have all the answers or are you comfortable with soliciting advice from your group and or a co-leader? The truth is, once you act, it is your decision regardless of where you get your information. I have noticed that novice guides often fall into the trap of thinking that they alone need to make their decisions without input. They are giving too much priority to concerns about their egos and reputations.

Part of a sound DMP includes using the information at your disposal at the time. The opinions and perspectives from group members can be an asset, or a liability, depending on their experience and expertise. If you do ask for advice, you will need to decide if it is valuable or not, and that can be difficult at times. I have heard very self-assured participants spout facts that were far from the truth. I have also received fantastic advice from some very shy, soft-spoken clients. In fact, on one occasion I had to pry an opinion out of one of them, which gave me a great perspective on the situation. If time permits, I tend to use participants that I have assessed as assets, when I need to discuss options. If it is a decision that will affect the well-being of the group, I will gather the group to discuss the options and get their feedback, if I have the luxury of time.

Decisions With Co-leaders
A co-leader is a blessing - most of the time. However, conflicting values, experiences, philosophies, lenses and styles, can be a real challenge if the two of you are stuck in your ways. If you can make your collective differences complement each other, you can have a win-win situation.

There needs to be give and take among your differences. Splitting responsibilities, to one's strengths, is one way to start. Having two brains making a decision may take a bit more time, but it will probably be a richer decision because you will be using more lens-factors. Of course, our different factors and styles can cause friction or delays if you let it.

The leader, who is designated to make immediate and/or final decisions, should be decided before the trip begins. The last thing a group needs is to have its two leaders arguing about what to do in an emergency. Before my trip leaders went off, I chose which one of them would have authority of the "final say" in emergency situations. My choice was mostly based on their first-aid and emergency training, in addition to my judgment of their past performances. I suggest you and your co-leader do the same. This split doesn't have to be reserved for emergency situations only. You can decide

which one of you will be the *Head Honcho* in charge of the
following:
- Emergencies;
- Meals;
- Navigation;
- First aid;
- Inter-group conflict;
- Logistics and itineraries (setting up and breaking camp);
- Equipment Maintenance.

Regardless of how you split your responsibilities, it is critical
that you do not disagree or argue in front of the group. It is
perfectly fine to go off to the side to discuss a matter quietly.
When I have done so with my co-leader, oftentimes a
member of the group yells out, "What are you guys talking
about?" My standard reply, done with a big smile, is "We are
trying to decide what to get you for your birthday." Once we
return to the group, one of us will say, "We needed to discuss
some leader stuff" or something along those lines.

Never hesitate to have private leader discussions. Just
because you split your responsibilities, it doesn't mean the
other leader ignores the areas that are not assigned to them.
Be ready to jump in if needed, because both of you are
collectively responsible for the entire trip. However, if there
needs to be a final say, your pre-trip designated authority
should be honored.

Something else to consider when co-leading is developing
your own sign language or signaling mechanisms,
specifically to avoid critical situations. One leader may be
close enough to avert a situation, but they are not watching
because it might be behind them. A quick signal from you
may be the proactive decision that is needed.

I have to say, it is an absolute joy to have a co-leader when
you both are in sync. It makes the trip easier and the group
gets more out of your individual strengths.

If you need to split the group, for whatever reason, here are some words of advice. The leaders need to be careful to not promise something to one group that will affect the other group, without input from the others. At times we use two vans to get to our destination. The leader in van 1 should not be making promises that exclude the input from those in van 2. Your goal is to avoid starting an "us" vs. "them" mentality before your destination. You are all one group and you are both leaders of that group. Having the sub-groups eating together at rest stops, intermingling, is a nice way of avoiding this issue.

Participants
You are a participant if you are a member of the group. As such, you have responsibilities to the other members, yourself and to the leaders if the trip is guided.

Responsibility To The Leaders
When you are on a trip, you see your guide doing so many things that you don't think about their primary purpose for being there. It is easy to get accustomed to being taken care of, especially if the guide seems to be doing everything. I think it is important for any participant to understand a guide's primary responsibilities. They include:
- Maintaining an acceptable level of risk throughout the trip;
- Trying to avoid dangerous situations;
- Dealing with accidents, illnesses and emergency situations;
- Managing and leading the group according to a specific itinerary;
- Being a resource for the participants;
- Providing the opportunity for an enjoyable time.

There are other responsibilities, such as: meals, cleaning, equipment management and education, which are icing on the cake. However, it is the primary ones, the "cake" itself, that are most important, so be mindful that your actions do not cause your leaders to lose focus on them.

As you can see, a leader has a lot on their plate. Helping your leader carry that plate is a lot better than being a big weight on that plate. I can only add, my hat goes off to all the volunteer guides and instructors who give of their time and expertise, for no monetary compensation.

Since all of us become participants in a group, at one time or another, I want to add a few more ways to make the experience easier for the leaders and more enjoyable for the group. If you ask, "Why should I make life easier for the leader?" my reply is simple. Since the group leader has so many responsibilities, as discussed above, I would think you would want them to be ready (physically and mentally) to identify and deal with potential emergencies rather than having to deal with members who need constant attention. Being a conscientious participant, who is asset to the group, requires less time and energy on the part of the leader.

How to be an asset to your group:
- Listen to and follow instructions;
- Do not turn off your brain because there is a leader;
- Be proactive in managing your own safety;
- Keep a watchful eye on your fellow participants;
- Pitch in and do more than your fair share;
- Stay within eye or earshot of the leader;
- Inform the leader if you wish to explore;
- If you are naturally loud, turn down the volume;
- Go with the flow of your environment, not against it;
- When in doubt, check with the leader.

If you are a paddler you may appreciate an article I wrote for my website called, *"The Group Paddling Creed."* Go to www.useakayak.org to view the article in the *Reflections from the Cockpit* link.

Even though you have a guide, you still need to take care of yourself. They are there to "guide" you - not take care of you. Your well-being should be your primary responsibility, even if it is high on their list. Remember, you are just one in the group, and their responsibility is the entire group. If something the leader says seems questionable, speak up. "I should have spoken up" will be of little use after the fact. Take charge of your life, within the parameters of the trip guidelines.

Groups

Just to be clear, I define a group as two or more participants. I can honestly say, whenever I went on day or overnight trips, with my buddies, I never thought of it as a group trip, even though it was. In addition, we never had a designated leader. We were just a bunch of friends sharing an adventure. In our case, we knew each other's strengths and we shared the responsibilities. Serious decisions were made in collaboration. Since I had more medical and emergency training, I knew my friends would let me take charge if it were ever necessary.

Groups are formed in many ways; however, the main thing that all groups have in common is a shared goal. If there were no shared goal, there would be no reason for individuals to group up.

"Leaderless Groups" are comprised of participants that believe there is no designated leader, as is the case for many club, friends and informal meet-up trips. These groups function with cooperative leadership, which means everyone is a participant and a possible leader. I have already discussed the elemental concerns for leaders and participants. Here are some for these cooperative style groups.

The Group DMP

My greatest concern is the questionable efficiency of "Group Decision-Making." We have looked at how the DMP works for you. Here is what it would look like for a group. Let's say we have eight in this group and there is an event. Let us now assume at least one of the eight recognized the event and has shared it with the group. Now we have eight separate DMPs going on at the same time. Here are the steps of the "Group DMP" for this event with eight different lenses:

Event -It has been recognized and shared with the group.

Evaluation - Eight opinions on how important the event is and how quickly it needs to be acted upon. Considerably more input being gathered. Lots of information is gathered but who decides what input is relevant? If there is a debate, more time is added to the process.

Goals - Most likely more goals listed, with the possibility of one or more of them being conflicting. I see more potential debating time.

Options - Needles to say there will be more options to consider, which means more time involved.

Action - Is there one person who makes the final choice? If yes, how and when were they chosen? If not, how is the committee of eight going to make their choice?

Results - If the action is ever taken, who will monitor the results and make the adjustments, if necessary?

One of the important lessons I have learned, from my emergency training programs, is the need for one person to be in charge, to give directions. More than one person shouting out instructions does not work efficiently. This person is the one who keeps the situation from becoming chaos. Thcy need to know the assets available so they can direct their use. They also need to prioritize assets and needs. They do not have to do it alone. They can still get advice from the collective expertise of the group, if time allows. However, they will be the one directing voice.

It is painfully obvious the group DMP can be an incredibly lengthy and challenging process. It can work, if there is time for it. However, events that do require immediate actions need to be made by one person and not by a slow group process. Therefore, at the very least, a *"Situational Leader"* needs to be designated for immediate action items, for any group venturing into dynamic environments.

Shared or Multi-Leader Trips

As I said above, everyone is a possible leader. If you think about these cooperative trips, I believe it is naive to think there are no leaders. Someone had to have done something for this trip to even get off the ground. The trip announcement needs some basics details, such as: date, location, meeting times, possible routes and the person to notify if you want to participate. This trip organizer may not lead the actual trip, but for now, they are going to be seen as the *"One"* in charge. I imagine this trip idea probably started when a few friends were sitting around and one of them said, "Lets organize a group trip to generic location, a month from now, since we three have the time off." Once they agree on it, one of them will send out the notice to their other friends.

I think it is important for participants of these kinds of trips to understand there will be folks taking the lead on specific tasks rather than one all encompassing leader. In fact, I recommend being more proactive about it. Create a mindset that participants will be divvying up the responsibilities of the trip. This not only gives each participant a chance to take charge of an area of responsibility, it helps everyone know who to contact when they have questions about specific aspects of the trip. Therefore, aside from advertising the basic info, there can be a call for volunteers for the following responsibilities (situational leaders):
- Meals and cooking;
- Clean-up and Leave No Trace;
- Equipment logistics;
- Transportation;
- First Aid and emergency care;
- Maintaining the route (map & compass guru);
- Emergency management coordinator;

With the key areas of responsibility assigned, any immediate decisions regarding these areas now has one person empowered to act for the good of the group. If there is time for input from others, then the specific situational leader, responsible for that area, can decide if a group decision is necessary.

Regardless of how you divide the responsibilities, as shown above, here is a more comprehensive list of items and areas that should be addressed for any group outing:

- Designated situational leaders;
- Group participant's assets (individual's training, expertise, skills, experience, etc...);
- Group medical histories (including dietary restrictions);
- Medications needed, how to administer and their location;
- Group equipment;
- Itineraries;
- Emergency procedures (contacting help, evacuation, nearest hospital);
- First Aid provider;
- Transportation needs;
- Meals, cooking and clean-up;
- Establish a group DMP, before it is needed;
- Split decision protocols (does the group split into two?);
- Individual expectations.

Any group that gets together, I can assure you, each member has their own set of expectations of what they want from the trip. This is where I have seen the most group conflict. If someone has their heart set on a specific campsite, hot springs, waterfall, route, or any other particular desire, you can be sure it will surface. That is why I included it in the list above. If it is stated up front, friction and disappointment may be averted, if the group addresses these expectations before the trip begins.

Even though this is a group, your responsibilities as a participant still apply with even more emphasis placed on taking care of yourself. Even with designated situational leaders, you should not abdicate your risk awareness and management. In my experience as a participant of leaderless trips, I felt like we were a collection of people all doing our solo trips even though we were together. The overall awareness of the individuals appeared to be greater than those on organized trips that were being guided.

A tool that may be helpful for these leaderless trips is an adaption of the *Paddling Creed* I mentioned above. I have adjusted the creed to be generic for any group trip. You may wish to use it for your group outings, if you want to be proactive with respect to participant responsibilities. It is an excellent tool for establishing group and trip norms.

Group Participant Creed

When I choose to adventure with a group, I realize I have a certain responsibility to that group. I understand the group members can be on the trip for different reasons. Some of my personal desires and freedoms may have to take second place to the needs of the group. I always have the right to do adventures alone if I so choose. Therefore, when I choose to be with a group I will try to be an asset to that group by abiding to the following principles:

- I will stay with the group;
- I will be on time and ready to go;
- I will be properly equipped for the trip;
- My equipment will be functional and properly maintained;
- I will adequately dress for the environment;
- I will stay adequately hydrated and nourished;
- I will carry the recommended safety equipment;
- I will not put the group in harm's way;
- I will practice acceptable risk management for myself and others;
- I will communicate with the group if there is a problem or if I need to leave;
- I will do my fair share of the work;
- I will respect the quiet time of others;
- I will not over-techno others with my new toys.

As you can see from the information in this chapter, it gets more complicated when having to make decisions when dealing with groups. I am not suggesting this is bad. I just want you to be aware of some of the challenges you could be facing, when you are responsible for others or adventuring with others. As a leader I found, being clear about my responsibilities and separating them from group expectations, gave me a good focus when having to make my decisions. I recommend you do the same.

The DMP, as described in this book, works the same whether you are alone, leading others or participating in a group. The big difference is, there is more to consider and more people affected by your decisions. If you are not comfortable with these extra responsibilities, I suggest you avoid traveling with others. With respect to guiding, since I relish sharing my experience with others, especially in the outdoors, I personally believe the rewards are well worth the added responsibilities.

CHAPTER 10

PARTING THOUGHTS

After reading through the manuscript, I had some parting thoughts I wanted to share with you.

In the beginning I stated that no single book could tell you what to do in every situation because there are too many variables. As it says in the bible, "Give a person a fish and you feed them for a day. Teach them how to fish and you feed them for life." Telling someone exactly what to do in every situation is like giving them a fish. Teaching them a process for making decisions, regardless of the situation, is teaching them how to problem solve, which will serve them for life. By sharing my thoughts and experiences, I am hoping it has motivated you to examine your DMP for better results in the future.

Even if you do not use my camera-lens analogy in your process, it is important for you to know the basis (your rationale) you use for your decisions and actions.

One of the re-occurring themes of this book is clarifying and knowing your *lens-factors*. As I mentioned, your list of factors will have some differences compared to those of others. Regardless of what is on your list, your factors need to be working for you instead of sabotaging you. Take the time to really get to know them. Writing them down is the first step.

One of my goals was to give you more things to consider throughout your entire DMP. After all, you don't know - what you don't know. I trust you may now have a bit more to think about and consider before taking action. Also, don't forget to watch out for filters.

Another important theme is putting more energy into being proactive, so you don't get into the situation in the first place. There will always be reasons that necessitate reactive decisions. As I have shown, thinking ahead and mastering the *"what if"* game will greatly minimize the number of reactive decisions you will likely face. Being caught off-guard in the outdoors can easily be avoided, if you just think ahead and do your research.

I encourage you to learn as much as you can about the environment you are planning to visit. If you are leading and/or involved in a group outing, *"get to know your people."* I have always found local knowledge to be invaluable.

Planning is extremely important, as long as you keep your plans flexible. Your plan is a guideline; it should not dictate your actions. You are in charge of implementing the plan as you see fit. Remember, forcing or sticking to an itinerary has been the cause of many mishaps on adventures.

In case you were wondering, my dedication to my dad was referring to what I should wear when we went fishing together. Whenever I asked what to bring, my dad would say, "You can always take it off (if it was too warm), but you can never put it on (if you don't bring it)." It was my introduction to planning ahead. Thanks, dad!

Now that you finished the book, think back and see if you would have made some different decisions had you known this additional information. As for looking back, the importance of reflection cannot be over stated. It is truly the key to learning from your actions. Take time to unplug from this electronic world unless, of course, you are reading this as an e-book.

Before I finish I have a few questions for you.
- Did the book make you think about your own lens-factors?
- Did you think about the steps you take when making decisions?
- Do you have more items to consider for your DMP?
- Did you learn some things from the scenarios?

- Do you think this book will help you make better decisions in the future?

If you answer yes to any or all of these, I have accomplished my goals for writing this book.

I am always trying to learn and improve. Therefore, I would appreciate any and all feedback you may have regarding my book. I enjoy positive feedback as much as the next person, but constructive criticism (positive or negative) is greatly appreciated. With respect to feedback, I have always told my staff, "Honest feedback is a true gift." If you liked the book or specific parts, please tell me why? If you did not, I want to know what you didn't like and why? In addition, if you would like to see more things added or items removed, I would like to hear about that too.

Any and all feedback can be sent to **study@useakayak.org.** Since time is precious, thank you in advance if you do respond. As an incentive, if I use your feedback in the next edition, I will send you a complimentary copy if and when it gets printed.

If you did find this book to be of value to you, please tell a friend and/or write an on-line review. This book can be purchased from the USK Store via my website **www.useakayak.org**.

Thank you for reading my book.

APPENDIX 1

PACKING LISTS

I have four different packing lists included in this appendix (Day hike, overnight trip, day paddle and over night paddling trip). I have found packing lists to be invaluable. But just because you have it on the list, does not automatically mean you will bring it with you. The way I have learned to deal with that problem is using a double check system.

Before the trip, I put the items on my list into a convenient pile. As it goes on the pile I check it off. When I pack up the items, I put a line through the checkmark, which means it has been loaded into the car or is in the final pile I will be packing into my buddies' car. I do not mark an item until it is in the pile. All too often, I have checked it on the way to getting it for the pile, but got distracted along the way, which resulted in a checked item that was not in the pile. That is why I have the double check. I am sure the guy who forgot his sleeping bag in scenario # 11 wished he had this system. I hope it works for you.

I also save my packing lists and edit them after I return. This way I can eliminate items that I really didn't need and add items I wished I had brought along. By doing this, over the years, I now have reliable lists that fit my needs, for my different outings. I suggest you use them as a starting point for your own personal lists. Remember to adjust them after your trips, while your thoughts are fresh in your mind. Since I regularly pack a small journal, for trip reflections, I make notes at day's end regarding my lists. I even note how I feel about my meals and how my equipment is functioning.

Another benefit of being properly equipped means one less decision you will have to make due to being unprepared. Here are the checklists that work for me. Since we may have different preferences and needs, adjust these lists to your needs.

Day Hike Packing List

Daypack
Layered clothing
Appropriate footwear
Extra clothing layers
Rain/wind shell
Water
Food
Medications
Sunscreen
Repellents (insects & bears)
Visor/hat
Sunglasses w/strap
Watch
Swiss Army knife
Nylon cord (50ft)
Compass w/ signal mirror
Waterproof matches
Whistle
Space blanket
Hiking poles
Topo maps and trail guides
Waterproof headlamp
Cell &/or satellite phone w/battery back-up
Satellite locator beacon
GPS (if you prefer)
First Aid kit (w/water treatment tablets)
Camera, extra battery & memory cards
Binoculars
Leaf-size plastic bag

If you are planning an overnight adventure, then add these items to your day trip list. The big difference with respect to the number of nights will be the amount of food and fuel you will need. Some extra clothes may also be necessary depending on your preferences. I usually rotate between two different base layers. One set is being cleaned, while I wear the other. My lightweight base layers dry quickly.

Generic Overnight Packing List

Backpack
Tent
Sleeping bag, liner & pillow
Ground sleeping pad
Camp chair
Food
Clothing for multi-days
Wildlife proof containers
Stove, fuel, pots, matches
Mug & food bowl
Utensils
Leatherman tool
Sponge & cleaner
Water bottle
Water filter & collapsible water bottles
Tie downs, carabiners & clothespins
Tarps (2X) (1 over tent & 1 over kitchen)
Headlamp & extra batteries
Tent lamp & candle
Hammock
P-Bottle/towel
T.P. & scooper/matches
Chamois cloth/towel
Trash bags
Journals & books
Reading glasses
Passport (if needed)

Sea Kayaking Packing List - Day Trip

Kayak
Paddles (one-spare)
PFD (w/knife, whistle & nose clips)
Sprayskirt
Kayak buoyancy bags if needed
Paddle float & pump
Tow belt
Stirrup
Immersion clothing
Watch
Shore clothing
Foul weather gear
Footwear (land & water)
Extra clothing layers
Gloves &/or pogies
Water system
Food
Medications
Dry bags (as needed)
Net bag (for carrying gear)
Sunscreen
Repellents (insects & bears)
Visor/hat
Sunglasses w/strap
Compass (deck & orienteering)
Charts
Tide & current tables
Extra bungee cords
Waterproof light (night paddling)
Cell &/or satellite phone w/battery back-up
VHF Radio w/ batteries + charger
GPS
EPIRB/Satellite locator beacon
Cockpit cover
Sponge
Signal flares
Painter (bow line)
First Aid kit (w/water treatment tablets)

Repair kit
Leaf-size plastic bag
Cockpit bag (emergency necessities)
Utility knife
Fire starters
Kayak wheels
Camera
Binoculars
Money, credit cards & I.D.
Tie down straps (also bumper ties)
Red flag for kayak (while driving)
Cleaning racks (for the kayak)
Cable lock (for securing kayak)

If you are planning an overnight kayaking trip then add these items to your day trip list. The big difference with respect to the number of nights will be the amount of food and fuels you will need. Some extra clothes may also be necessary depending on your preferences. I usually rotate between two different base layers. One set is being cleaned while I wear the other. My lightweight base layers dry quickly.

Sea Kayaking Overnight Packing List

Tent
Sleeping bag, liner & pillow
Ground sleeping pad
Camp chair
Extra clothing
Personal hygiene items
Stove, fuel, pots, matches
Mug & food bowl
Swiss Army knife & utensils
Sponge & cleaners
Water bottles
Dry bags
Tie downs, carabiners & clothespins
Tarps (2X) (1 over tent & 1 over kitchen)
Headlamp & extra batteries
Camp lamp &/or candles
Water filter & collapsible water bottles
Hammock
Fishing gear
Saw &/or small axe
Sail or kite (if you use them)
P-Bottle/towel
T.P. & scooper/matches
Chamois cloth/towel
Trash bags
Journals & books
Reading glasses
Passport (if needed)

APPENDIX 2

MINIMIZING STRONG EMOTIONS

Most strong emotions happen quickly. It is triggered by an event. It means you have to try and deal with that event, while under the influence of those intense emotions, which can cloud your judgment and performance. The three emotions I have witnessed most often on trips are: fear, anger and loss (death or heartbreak).

When working on my Experiential Education degree, I learned some techniques for reducing and sometimes eliminating strong emotions. I have found the techniques useful for me; my students and I hope they work you.

Exaggerate the Emotion/Symptoms
Emotions are in your mind. However, they do manifest themselves with certain physical symptoms. I have found that dealing with the symptoms can actually affect the emotions in question.

Fear and anger can trigger adrenaline, which makes you feel like you are bursting at the seams. "Fight or Flight" it is a perfect example of that burst of energy. You will either run away or stand your ground, with intensity. Your goal is to get rid of the excess energy, if you want to regain control. The methods for dealing with fear and anger are the same.

Fear is the most common emotion people feel in outdoor settings, due to risk perception, facing the unknown and/or new challenges. Fear and anger usually manifest themselves in the following ways:
- Nervous inside;
- Shaking;
- Tense muscles;
- Altered breathing rate;
- Accelerated heart rare;
- Clenched Jaw;
- Desire to scream.

When you are shaking, feeling nervous inside, your muscles are tense, your ability to perform tasks decrease. Having a tense body negatively affects your balance, especially when sitting in a kayak. When your body is relaxed it can freely move as needed. Try walking on something narrower than your foot, with your body tense, and then try it relaxed. You can feel the difference. Here is an exercise I do with my beginning kayak students that illustrates my point about exaggeration.

Most beginners feel unstable when they first sit in a kayak. You can see their bodies tense-up and their kayaks begin twitching from side to side. One of the first drills I have them execute is properly holding their partner's kayak. While their kayak is being stabilized, I have them sit up on their back deck, which feels unstable compared to being in their seat. Then I have them stand on their seat, which feels even more unstable. After nervously standing up for ten seconds, they cannot wait to get back into their seats. Once they are back in their kayaks that initial instability they felt magically disappeared. After exaggerating their instability, their initial uneasiness seems fine in comparison.

When my stomach feels nervous I tighten my abdominal muscles for ten seconds and then let go. I repeat this at least ten times and more if I am really scared. This also helps reduce the tension in my torso. Sometimes I have to tense the entire body to reduce the nervousness. By tensing and releasing your muscles you are beginning to fatigue them. You are using up and reducing the emotional energy. Over time you will find out how long and how intense you need to contract you muscles, to get the results that work best for you.

I also use breathing exercises to get my breathing back to normal. I take very deep breaths, hold it for three seconds and then exhale slowly. I do that three times and then wait about thirty seconds and do it again, until my breathing rate is back to normal. If you begin to feel dizzy, go back to your normal breathing.

I have also found primordial screaming to be very affective, especially when I am angry. Doing some loud consecutive yelling will also help your breathing. Just think of screaming as a means of expelling your emotions, from your torso to the universe via your mouth.

Before I would go down a class V+ rapid, I would do a set of tensing drills, yell at the top of my lungs a few times and then execute a couple of rolls to reduce the tension in my body.

Intense exercise in any form will reduce the symptoms I mentioned above. Again, your goal is to reduce that built up energy.

As for dealing with loss, if there is anger included, then the methods above will be helpful. If it is a strong sense of sadness, melancholy or lack of motivation, exercise could also be your salvation. Aside from expending built up energy, exercise causes your body to produce endorphins, which could help lift your spirits. Spending at least thirty minutes of intense power walking, jogging, running, biking, paddling or swimming, could improve your mood.

When I am very sad and feel like crying, I don't hold back. In fact, I not only let myself cry, I try to cry uncontrollably. I try to think of all my losses and intensify the crying. When I am wept out, I feel a lot better. If you prefer not doing this aloud, try using a pillow for crying and/or screaming.

Whether you use my recommended methods or find ones of your own, your ultimate goal is to keep intense emotions from clouding your judgment, which ultimately leads to poor decisions.

APPENDIX 3

DECISION I WISH I COULD CHANGE

As I mentioned in an earlier chapter, I look at who I am today, as the sum total of all the decisions I have made in my life. I believe the overwhelming majority of my decisions have been positive, because when I look back on them, I am proud to share them, if asked. However, I am far from perfect. I have made very bad decisions and a few I am ashamed to even admit. The lessons I learned from my bad decisions, mistakes, regrets and my shameful ones taught me more than my successes. Even though I know this intellectually, I wish I could have a "Do-Over" on this one.

I was living in Santa Barbara, at age 27, when I received word my dad, age 51, had a heart attack. My wife and I got on the first plane back to New York City. We got there late in the evening. After stopping to see my mom I jumped in the car to pick up a few items from Dad's work that mom said I needed to get. I then went to the hospital even though my mom told me there were no visiting hours until morning.

I sat in the car outside the hospital (the same hospital where I was born) wondering if I should force my way in regardless of official hours. I decided I would wait because I didn't want to disturb my dad, thinking I will see him after he had a good night's sleep.

The next morning, as we were getting ready to leave the house, a call came in that he took a turn for the worse. When we got to the hospital we were told my father had died. I later found out, they didn't want to tell us over the phone my dad had died, so on the way I still had my hopes up that I would see him and he would survive.

To this day, I regret not going in to see my dad the night before. I never got the chance to tell him I loved him and speak with him one last time. Knowing him, he would have wanted reassurances that I would make sure mom would be cared for, which she was. I had no concept how much my decision would haunt me throughout my life. The impact was profound.

However, there is a positive side to my regret. It encouraged me to develop future hindsight. I also take every opportunity to tell the ones I care about how much they mean to me. Since I travel often, I frequently tell close friends and family, "If anything happens during the trip, know I love you." Even though this event has, in the long run, helped me make what I believe to be higher quality decisions, I would still trade it, to have that last moment with my dad.

I have shared this specific hindsight episode with many people. Many of them have thanked me, because it prompted them to make an effort when faced with somewhat similar circumstances.

I am sharing my experience with you, to encourage you to think about what is really important in your life, because losing it will likely have a significant impact. To find out what really matters, just answer this question, "How will I feel if I lost...?" It could be a family member, a pet, a job, an object, one of your senses, your mobility, etc...

Regardless of your answer, I suggest you appreciate "**it**" while you still have it and remember **it's** importance when making decisions. You may also wish to identify actions you can take now, that may help you find closure after the loss.

Index

A

Action
  action, 48, 71
  default action, 50
  immediate, 67
  non-action, 48
  postponed, 68
Adventure, 123-128
Anticipation, 64
Armchair Quarterback, 3

B

Before you go, 129-142

C

Clothing/layering, 132
Compromise, 60

D

Decision-Making Lens, 4-38
  focusing lens, 32
  lens-factors, 5-32
  lens filters, 35
Decision-Making Process, 39-74
Decision-Making Process Reactive, 39-62
  action, 48
  evaluate, 42
  event, 40
  goals, 44
  options, 46
  results, 53
Decision-Making Process Proactive, 63-74
  action, 71
  evaluate, 70
  event, 64
  goals, 70
  immediate action, 67
  options, 70

postponed action, 68
results, 71
Decision I wish I could change, 172

E
Evaluation, 42, 70
Event, 40, 64
  events vs. conditions, 41
  multiple events, 41
  potential event, 64
  pre-event alert, 65
  recognizing events, 40
Exposure, 130
  dehydration, 136
  hyperthermia, 134
  hypothermia, 130
  nutrition, 136

F
Fail safe, 52

G
Goals, 48, 70
Groups, 143-159, 154
  assessing group, 145
  expectations of group, 146
  group decision-making process, 154
  group participants creed, 158
  leaderless trips, 154
  shared or multi-leaders, 156
  situational leader, 155

H
Heat loss, 131-134
  conduction, 131
  convection, 132
  evaporation, 132
  radiation, 131
  respiration, 132

J

Judgment, 1-3
   definitions, 1
   good and poor judgment, 2
   snap judgments, 51

L

Leaders, 143-159
   assessing group, 145
   co-leaders, 150
   decision-making style, 148
   expectations of group, 146
   expectations of leaders, 143
   shared or multi-leaders, 156
   situational leader, 155
Lens (Decision-making), 4-38
   focusing lens, 32
   lens-factors, 5-32
   lens filters, 35
Lost, 137-138
   mental state, 137
   signaling, 137

M

Mistakes, 58-60
Minimizing strong emotions, 169

N

Necessary equipment, 138-142

O

Options, 46, 70

P

Packing lists, 163-168
   day hike list, 164
   day paddle list, 166
   overnight hike list, 165
   overnight paddle list, 168

Participants, 143-159, 152
  group participants creed, 158
  responsibilities, 152
Parting thoughts, 160
Pointing fingers, 59

R
Reflection, 61
Results, 53, 71
Risk assessment, 123-128
  Risk questionnaire, 125

S
Safe/safety, 123-128
Scenarios, 75-82, 83-122
  #1 Head wound, 75, 83
  #2 Huge surf, 76, 84
  #3 Group dissent, 76, 85
  #4 Bike accident, 76, 87
  #5 Cave kayaking, 77, 89
  #6 Trip location Change, 77, 90
  #7 Equipment failure, 77, 91
  #8 Behind schedule, 77, 93
  #9 Snow slope, 78, 94
  #10 Emergency stop, 78, 96
  #11 No sleeping bag, 78, 97
  #12 Different agendas, 78, 98
  #13 Accidental death, 79, 100
  #14 Bickering couple, 79, 101
  #15 Canyon flash flood, 79, 102
  #16 Seasick paddler, 80, 105
  #17 Surf zone capsize, 80, 107
  #18 Sudden fog, 81, 109
  #19 Shark in the area, 81, 111
  #20 Slow paddler, 81, 112
  #21 No tidal or current tables, 81, 114
  #22 Capsize in strong current, 81, 115
  #23 Panicked swimmer, 81, 116
  #24 Cold & wet paddler, 82, 119
  #25 Flying kayak, 82, 121

T
Trip planning, 72

U
Use it or lose it, 55

ABOUT THE AUTHOR

Wayne Horodowich learned his core survival skills having spent the first 24 years of his life in New York City. Little did he know that growing up in the projects in Brooklyn would help him prepare for his life as an adventure educator. As a 6'7" college varsity basketball player, he ended up being a basketball instructor/counselor at a summer camp where he discovered his passion for teaching. Wayne graduated with a B.S. in Physical Education from City College of New York (CCNY) and immediately began teaching there. While still in NY he became a certified Scuba instructor and a downhill ski instructor, which provided the opportunity to lead diving trips to Jamaica and teach skiing classes in New Jersey.

After teaching at CCNY for two years, he headed west for graduate school at the University of Oregon where he earned his first Master's degree in Anatomy & Physiology and spent the next year working on his PhD in Bio Mechanics. Instead of finishing his Doctoral work, Wayne decided to accept a Lecturer position at the University of California in Santa Barbara (UCSB).

Before leaving Oregon, he took a month long Mountaineering Course through Pacific Northwest Outward Bound Schools, in the Three Sister Wilderness Area of the Oregon Cascades, where he learned his core wilderness skills. Wayne regularly credits the Outward Bound program for teaching him that almost all of his limitations are self-imposed.

Wayne's first four years at UCSB were spent teaching Anatomy, Physiology, First Aid & CPR and fitness classes. On the side, he taught Scuba diving and began utilizing his newly acquired wilderness skills backpacking, mountaineering and rock climbing. In addition, he would lead an occasional trip for the University's outdoor program. Somewhere in there, he managed to get his EMT certification.

179

Due to some life challenges in 1980, Wayne left full time lecturing and assumed the Director's position for UCSB's Adventure Programs, which he continued to manage for 25 years. With the invaluable help from incredible professional and student staff, the program grew exponentially. What began as a six trip per quarter program, developed to be one that offered 30 - 40 offerings per quarter and added an indoor Team Building/Challenge Course and two indoor climbing walls. Wayne feels his greatest accomplishment was the Leadership Training Course (LTC), where he trained UCSB students to be trip leaders and instructors. It started with a handful of students being trained each quarter. The LTC program expanded to a five-month training course with about 40 - 60 student trainees per year.

Not liking to sit still, Wayne continued his personal growth by pursuing his second Master's in Experiential Education at UCSB. He also expanded his outdoor skills to include: PSIA Ski Instructor, backcountry skiing, certified avalanche training, river canoeing, swift-water rescue, certified instructor in sea and whitewater kayaking and challenge course training. He even found time to compete in surf kayaking and eventually became the captain of the US Surf Kayaking Team, which competed in the world championships in Thurso, Scotland in 1991 and Santa Cruz, California in 1993.

As the years went by, sea kayaking became Wayne's sport of choice because he was able to combine all of the skills he had learned from scuba diving, backpacking, skiing, canoeing and mountaineering and use them for kayaking. Being a professional educator it was easy for him to get involved in the sea kayaking clinic and lecture circuit. When the world-wide-web became viable, Wayne finally had the means to fulfill his vision for a global resource for sea kayaking education. In 2000 he established the University of Sea Kayaking (USK), which included: a comprehensive educational website, an In-Depth Instructional Video Series, symposia presentations and on-water clinics taught domestically and internationally.

In 2005 Wayne took an early retirement from UCSB, at age 55, and headed to the Pacific Northwest where he continued to produce instructional videos and write articles. He presently enjoys traveling around North America in his converted van: teaching clinics, giving presentations, visiting friends and spending time in the great outdoors feeding his soul. His passion is still teaching, which was the motivation for writing this book. Wayne wanted to share his years of experience: training over 1,000 trip leaders, leading over 1,000 trips/classes, enjoying numerous personal adventures, 33 years of college teaching, and his life's successes and mistakes, with the hopes of helping others when faced with difficult decisions while on adventures or in life.

Write your list of lens-factors here

*Visit the University of Sea Kayaking website
www.useakayak.org for books and articles by Wayne
Horodowich*

and

*USK's award winning "In-Depth" Instructional
Video series for sea kayaking*

USK's motto:

"Do it in a way that works best for you!"

The secrets to being self-reliant in a survival situation are in preparation before you leave home. *How to Think Like a Survivor* reveals simple ways to overcome the unexpected in the outdoors.

Tom Watson helps you learn how to think through potential emergency situations - stressing the "why" behind processes and procedures, not merely learning what to do and how to do it - all towards finding solutions to avoid disaster in the wilderness. Tom's book is available on Amazon, through his website: https://tomoutdoors.com/writingphoto-recognition/

If you like adventure then I highly recommend this book.

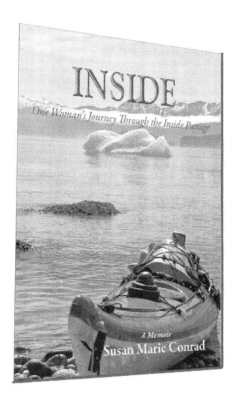

Inside, One Woman's Journey Through the Inside Passage is a rip-roaring true-life adventure story of Susan Conrad's 1,200-mile solo sea kayak expedition from Anacortes, Washington to Juneau, Alaska. It's also a candid and intimate account of how Susan faced her inward fears and outward challenges which ultimately led to a journey of self-discovery. Learn more at SusanMarieConrad.com or contact the author directly at susan@susanmarieconrad.com

Now it is your turn to choose wisely!